Off-Track Profs

Off-Track Profs

Nontenured Teachers in Higher Education

John G. Cross and Edie N. Goldenberg

The MIT Press
Cambridge, Massachusetts
London, England

For information about special quantity discounts, please email special_sales@mitpress.mit.edu.

This book was set in Sabon by SNP Best-set Typesetter Ltd., Hong Kong. Printed and bound in the United States of America.

Library of Congress Cataloging-in-Publication Data

Cross, John G.
Off-track profs: nontenured teachers in higher education / John G. Cross and Edie N. Goldenberg.
   p. cm
Includes bibliographical references and index.
ISBN 978-0-262-01291-1 (hardcover : alk. paper). 1. College teachers—Tenure—United States. 2. College teachers—Employment—United States. I. Goldenberg, Edie N. II. Title.
LB2335.7.C76   2009
378.1′214—dc22

                                                              2008042149

10 9 8 7 6 5 4 3 2 1

Contents

Preface

From reading newspapers and education surveys, it is easy to infer that higher education is in trouble. Graduate student teaching assistants and non-tenure-track (NTT) faculty are joining unions; new PhDs are often frustrated in their searches for tenure-track positions; tenured faculty feel greater pressures than ever before to produce cutting-edge scholarship instead of teaching beginning undergraduates; legislators demand accountability in undergraduate education at the same time that they provide less of the funding needed to support it; and universities themselves, convinced somehow that only the business sector knows how to manage large and complex enterprises, are turning in increasing numbers to untested and often inappropriate internal "business models" that have nothing to do with the objectives or values of the academic enterprise. We hear increasingly that PhDs in untenured or part-time positions are exploited, and it has become popular to characterize them as contingent faculty—a demeaning term that deprives them of the status and respect that is normally accorded to college faculty. This general malaise has had its impact on administrators as well: Turnover among academic leaders has increased in recent years, as conflicts among administrators and between administrators and the faculty abbreviate supportable terms in office.

As academic administrators at the University of Michigan, we observed all of these developments with concern. In our roles as dean and associate dean of the College of Literature, Science and the Arts (LSA), we routinely reviewed our own operations and compared ourselves with other liberal arts colleges within large research universities. One of our greatest surprises from those reviews was the growth in numbers of non-tenure-track (NTT) instructors teaching undergraduates at Michigan and at other leading research universities.

This growth in numbers seemed to have a life of its own. We became convinced that we needed a much deeper understanding of the processes for hiring faculty and the reasons for hiring faculty who are ineligible for tenure. The active debates about growth in the numbers of NTT faculty appeared to us to be unduly narrow and negative. Claims that university administrators set out intentionally to save money by hiring less expensive teachers and then further to exploit them by extracting many hours of instruction in return for paltry wages, no benefits, job insecurity, and second-class status simply did not accurately describe what we felt to be true at Michigan or elsewhere. We decided to explore this further in an effort to explain what was happening to university employment practices and to offer some insights into the implications of these trends for the future of higher education. To do this, we needed a wider sample of universities than just our own, even as we restricted that sample to universities comparable to ours in terms of their strong commitments to academic research.

We knew that this sort of undertaking would require detailed knowledge of the internal structure and procedures of each university in our sample—especially in light of the fact that no two universities seemed to use the same definitions and descriptions for their teaching resources. Moreover, we were not certain that we could gain sufficient access to enough distinguished universities to construct a set of cases that would permit valid generalizations. Therefore, we began with a planning grant from the Andrew W. Mellon Foundation during 2001–02 to study four universities (one of which was our own) and assess the feasibility of the overall project. This set of four was composed of Research I institutions that are similar in terms of both their research status and their competitiveness for faculty and students. At the same time, we sought institutions with structural characteristics that vary in ways that should affect academic personnel policies. Accordingly, the three institutions that we added led to a set of four that contained two public and two private universities; two institutions in large labor markets and two in areas with more limited workforce availability; and two institutions that have adopted highly decentralized budgeting systems (responsibility-centered management) and two that have not.

After developing summary profiles of each university, we visited their campuses. Our goals were (1) to gather institutional data on the instructional mix of tenure-track, non-tenure-track, and graduate student teaching assistants over time (and by discipline and level of instruction) and discuss the data to understand their meaning; (2) to interview knowledgeable administrators and faculty to understand hiring and budget processes and the reasons for employing NTT instructors; and (3) to explore implications of hiring NTT employees for union movements, governance, academic freedom, and university functioning.

Our colleagues on these campuses were generous with their time and insights. They shared our interest in the issues and encouraged us to pursue them further. This level of success led the Andrew W. Mellon Foundation to provide generous support for an expansion to a total of ten universities, all members of the Association of American Universities and all similar in research status and competitiveness for faculty and students. At the same time, we tried to select universities that would differ in ways that might influence faculty personnel practices: public versus private institutions, locations in large versus small labor markets, and institutions with centralized versus highly decentralized budgeting systems.

We hope that those who read this book will come away with a deeper understanding of the instructional hiring processes on our nation's premier research campuses—including why hiring trends look the way they do, why we should care about them, and what can usefully be done to prevent potential problems from arising. We also hope that others come to share our sense that hiring practices provide a fascinating window on decision making in higher education. Finally, this work is motivated by a belief that American universities are important national assets that are worth preserving, protecting, and strengthening but that pursuit of this goal requires a more complete understanding of the complexities of these institutions than can be obtained from newspaper reports or surveys that generalize across a multiplicity of dissimilar settings.

J.G.C.
E.N.G.

Acknowledgments

Our project benefited from the advice and cooperation of a large number of people. Of course, none of them bears responsibility for any errors on our part. We developed our interest in the changing character of the professoriate during our time as dean and associate dean of the College of Literature, Science and the Arts at the University of Michigan. We learned a great deal during that decade from department chairs, associate chairs, provosts, associate provosts, presidents, fellow deans, technical staff, and others in Ann Arbor as well as from other deans in the CIC and the Association of American Universities. We want to give special thanks to colleagues at Michigan who gave us substantial insight and assistance, including James Duderstadt, Anthony (Rick) Francis, Philip Hanlon, Helene McCarren, Peter Steiner, Charles Yocum, Lori Haskins, Michael Cohen, David Dobbie, Kirsten Fogh Herold, Jon Curtis, Edward Gramlich, Gilbert Whitaker, Bonnie Halloran, Ian Robinson, Louise August, Jeanne Miller, and Carol Hollenshead.

We thank the Andrew W. Mellon Foundation and especially William Bowen and Harriet Zuckerman, who believed in our effort, funded it, and encouraged us along the way. We also acknowledge the support of the Department of Political Science, the Gerald R. Ford School of Public Policy at the University of Michigan, and four able research assistants—Clint Peinhardt, Keith Rainwater, Kathleen Tipler, and especially Kharis Templeman.

We received detailed comments on our manuscript from some of those mentioned above as well as from Ernst Benjamin, Morton Lowengrub, Ronald Ehrenberg, Jack Schuster, Nancy Weiss Malkiel, and several anonymous reviews for the MIT Press. We thank them, but take all responsibility for any errors. We thank the many colleagues at the University of Illinois who made time for us, especially Jessie Delia, who helped organize our visit to Champagne-Urbana; we thank many colleagues at the University of Washington, with special thanks to Lee Huntsman, David Hodge, Susan Jeffords, Phillip Hoffman, and Debra Friedman; we thank many colleagues at the University of Virginia, with special thanks to Gene Block, Edward Ayers, Gertrude Fraser, David Brenneman; we thank colleagues at the University of California and the Berkeley campus, with special mention of Robert Berdahl, George Breslauer, M.R.C. Greenwood, Ralph Hexter, Clayton Heathcock, Michael Mascuch, David Moers, Richard Newton, and Geoffrey Owen; we thank our colleagues at Washington University, with special thanks to Mark Wrighton and Edward Macias; we thank our colleagues at Duke University, with special thanks to Richard Brodhead, William Chafe, Nannerl Keohane, Peter Lange, Leigh DeNeef, and various professors of the practice; we thank our colleagues at MIT, with special mention of Charles Vest, Susan Hockfield, Robert Brown, Philip Khoury, Thomas Magnanti, Robert Redwine, Robert Silbey, Lydia Snover, and John Curry; we thank our colleagues at Cornell, with special mention of Hunter Rawlings, Biddy Martin, Jeffrey Lehman, Walter Cohen, Michael Matier, and Kathleen Gemmell; we thank our colleagues at Northwestern, with special mention of Lawrence Dumas, Michael Dacey, Barbara O'Keefe, John Birge, Eric Sundquist, and Adair Waldenberg.

We also want to express our appreciation for assistance from the American Association of University Professors, Phyllis Franklin and the Modern Language Association, the Coalition on the Academic Workforce, and the Association of American Universities. We both enjoyed working with the staff at the MIT Press. Finally, we benefited tremendously from the support, insights, and encouragement of friends and family—Cynthia Cross, Edith Fine, Mary Ann Ritter, and Eleanor Singer.

1

Do We Know Who Teaches Our Students?

Elite research universities in the United States are revered around the world. International students come to the United States to study; academics overseas send their students here; outstanding faculty from across the globe choose to spend their careers as professors in the United States; universities in Asia, Europe, South America, and Africa seek partnerships and exchanges with U.S. institutions; and leaders in higher education from other countries visit to learn how our universities function as they strive to emulate the successes of world-class institutions in this country. We have achieved a position of global leadership in higher education, an important national asset.

Over time, significant changes can be seen in the missions of our best universities as well as in their operations, staffing, and leadership, but the tenured faculty and many university leaders seem largely oblivious to them. Today, outstanding teacher-scholars spend much more of their time and energy on their individual scholarly work and their national and international networks than they spend on their local institutions. They enjoy tremendous independence and considerable control over their job duties and arrangements. If local conditions sour, professors in highly ranked departments can relocate, and they do (although not always to comparable institutions). Meanwhile, few attend to matters of institutional health, governance, or academic freedom. With increasing competition for excellence in higher education coming from universities in other lands, will ours retain their high status even as changes in the makeup of the faculty are ignored by faculty members, provosts, and presidents? In writing this book, we seek to highlight important trends in the nature of the faculty and issues that we believe need to be addressed by those committed to maintaining the high quality of our best research institutions.

At the same time they are envied from abroad, U.S. research universities are attacked at home, and criticisms are nowhere more frequent and pointed than in the area of undergraduate education. Challenges come in many forms: research universities emphasize research to the neglect of undergraduate teaching;[1] research universities promote political correctness by hiring faculty who promote extreme or one-sided views in their instruction;[2] universities exploit "contingent faculty" and graduate students by engaging in bait-and-switch tactics that advertise high institutional standing based on distinguished faculty whom undergraduates rarely meet.[3] Worse yet, low-cost faculty substitutes may not speak or understand English well enough to be effective in the classroom.[4] The high and increasing cost of a college degree adds to public dissatisfaction with college experiences that seem inadequate.[5]

While we do not agree with most of these criticisms, we take them seriously and believe that they need to be addressed.[6] To address them effectively, we need to understand both the forces at work on university campuses today that affect academic priorities and incentives as well as the levers of change. Those forces are complex. Our project in this book is to clarify them and to stimulate serious discussion about the implications of those forces for the future of our nation's leading research universities.

Most critics of higher education tend to make two flawed assumptions. They assume that a conventional administrative hierarchy is in place on campus and that those at the top are intentionally producing undesirable outcomes. These critics blame the misplaced priorities of university leaders for the shortcomings in undergraduate education. University leaders are urged to change their priorities with the expectation that better undergraduate experiences will follow.

Yet anyone with experience leading a university understands that the reality is much more complicated than that. Presidents may be the most influential people on campus, but their influence is severely limited. Merely changing their priorities will not ensure organizational change. This is so for a number of reasons that we explore in this book. First, university information systems are inadequate for administrative decision making. Presidents lack information about fundamental aspects of their institutions and lack the means to track instructional changes or evaluate education policies. Second, presidents come and go. They and their principal lieutenants rarely stay in place long enough to change fundamental aspects of their institutions. Third, universities operate in an intensely competitive world that severely limits what any one can do without suffering a loss in stature. Those universities with the greatest resources and reputations may appear to be well positioned to break from the pack, but even their resources and reputations are vulnerable to competition. Fourth, universities are strikingly decentralized institutions. As Cohen and March aptly observed more than thirty years ago in their study of forty-one colleges and universities, "Academic 'policy' is the accretion of hundreds of largely autonomous actions taken for different reasons, at different times, under different conditions, by different people."[7] In this environment, structural changes, introduced with the best of intentions, can sometimes encourage subordinates to take actions that accumulate into patterns of behavior that are diametrically opposed to presidential aims.

The second flawed assumption is that national averages can be applied to individual institutions. Take, for example, widespread criticism of the working conditions of non-tenure-track faculty on campus.[8] Much of what is written relies on national studies of college faculty,[9] and the conclusions do not always ring true for our nation's elite universities. The itinerant lecturer who teaches individual courses on multiple campuses for paltry wages and no benefits does reflect reality in some places[10] but is virtually unknown on elite research campuses. Their leaders can dismiss complaints about the growing numbers and poor treatment of non-tenure-track faculty as something happening elsewhere—only in public institutions as a consequence of state budget crises or mainly in the rapidly growing community college or for-profit sectors.

Who are the faculty who teach undergraduates on these select campuses, and what are their employment arrangements? One of the major surprises of our study is that nobody seems to know. A number of reports of national data collected by the U.S. Department of Education provide summaries that break down total faculty numbers into tenure-track and non-tenure-track categories by type of institution, by specific university, and by discipline.[11] These studies provide a general picture of trends, although we make the case that they all likely understate the number of individuals who are off the tenure track who teach undergraduates in the university as a whole. They are unable to break out those categories by school or college within universities, however, and that limits their ability to characterize the faculties responsible for most of the undergraduate education on campus. Knowing who is teaching undergraduates and understanding how they engage with their students are important because the faculty bears primary responsibility for the quality of undergraduate education. The faculty offers classes, establishes the curriculum, sets graduation requirements, and shares in university governance.

We focus in this book on faculty members in distinguished research universities—public and private—in arts and sciences and engineering, the two schools with the largest undergraduate enrollments. We do not assume that the processes at work in large, elite, and relatively well-funded research universities are identical to those at work in other types of institutions of higher education. We know they are not. However, we do believe that these universities are especially important because they give U.S. higher education its high international standing, they are emulated by other institutions, and they are best positioned to strike out in new directions when warranted. They are also the least likely to pursue policies that diminish the role of tenure or tenured faculty—in part because they are busy trying to attract and retain the most distinguished people in each field and in part because their administrators recognize that their reputations for listening to the faculty are important in those efforts. As such, elite research universities provide a strong test case of resistance to pressures to increase numbers of instructors outside of the traditional boundaries of tenure. And they also happen to be the universities that we know best.

We became interested in this topic while serving as academic administrators at the University of Michigan. In our roles as dean and associate dean of the College of Literature, Science, and the Arts (LSA), we launched an initiative in 1990 to revitalize the educational experiences of undergraduates at Michigan, and we realized considerable success. Our senior faculty members were willing and even eager to reengage with first-year students in small seminars and with sophomore students in undergraduate research experiences. Nonetheless, we quickly realized how little we knew about the makeup of own faculty. We routinely reviewed our own operations and collected data about LSA and similar arts and sciences colleges at universities that we regarded as peers. Generally, those data painted a familiar picture, but in one important instance we were surprised: we never anticipated the significant increase over time in employment of part-time and full-time non-tenure-track instructors in our own college. Our office was entrusted with academic appointment policy, and yet we observed substantial growth in a type of appointment that we never consciously decided to make. The expanding role of non-tenure-track instructors was taking place under our noses but without our being fully aware of it. We were also surprised to learn about some of the employment circumstances of lecturers in our college that were established in departments without our participation.[12]

Anecdotal evidence suggested that other leading universities were having the same experience, and although several colleges (including our own) had attempted to implement policies that would rationalize the use of non-tenure-track instructors, none had met with much success. We realized that leaders of elite universities with responsibility for undergraduate education generally lack adequate understanding of central features of the undergraduate experiences at their own institutions. They do not fully understand why universities engage in particular instructional hiring practices, and they do not comprehend the consequences of those practices for the quality of educational experiences, the functioning of the university, or the excellence of the academic environment.

As social scientists, we became intrigued by this conundrum. We decided to explore these matters at Michigan and elsewhere. We believed that understanding educational operations is an essential first step in designing successful, sustainable reforms for improvement in undergraduate education. We have also come to appreciate that instructional hiring decisions provide a fascinating window into how elite universities operate. These decisions, taken one by one, accumulate and determine the makeup of the faculty, and that makeup may be very different from what anyone intends.

Our purposes in this book are four—first, to describe the instructional workforce and the trends in hiring in arts and sciences and in engineering at our nation's premier universities; second, to understand what drives these patterns and trends; third, to explain why we should care about this if we want to improve undergraduate education, support collegiality on campus, trust in faculty governance, protect tenure, and preserve our preeminence in higher education across the globe; and finally, to offer university leaders some suggestions for how they might address these issues.

With support from the Andrew W. Mellon Foundation, we selected ten universities, all outstanding Research I institutions that are similar in terms of both their research status and their competitiveness for faculty and students. Five are public: the University of California–Berkeley, University of Illinois, University of Michigan, University of Virginia, and University of Washington. Four are private: Duke University, the Massachusetts Institute of Technology, Northwestern University, and Washington University. One, Cornell University, is a mixed public-private institution. We sought institutions with contextual and structural characteristics that vary in ways that we expected would affect academic personnel policies. We included institutions in large labor markets and in areas with more limited workforce availability; we included institutions that have adopted highly decentralized budgeting systems (responsibility-centered management) and some that have not.

We began close to home. We were fortunate that Michigan had a relatively well-developed management information system. Even so, tracking the numbers of non-tenure-track instructors we employed was challenging, and our subsequent efforts to rationalize and limit the hiring of lecturers in our college met with only partial success.[13] As we sought information about hiring practices in other universities, we learned that few collect data in a form that can be used to monitor non-tenure-track appointments. Some use staff titles for instructors, some use faculty titles for staff, and some limit the title of "faculty" to tenure-track faculty (meaning that instructors off the tenure track appear in none of their faculty data reports). Even when the data are available, the definitions across universities differ, making comparisons suspect. To get a comprehensive view of instructional employment practices that would permit comparison and genuine understanding, we decided it was necessary to review the internal structure and procedures of each institution and find (or define) categories of comparable instructional types.

Discussions with our peers at other institutions convinced us that provosts and deans often lack adequate information to support appropriate hiring of faculty to provide undergraduate instruction. We have all heard departments argue for additional tenure-track or tenured hires because of the press of undergraduate enrollments. Yet we do not always know who is actually teaching our students, and we cannot compare the teaching effectiveness of different categories of instructor—that is, we cannot provide credible evidence that part-time or full-time non-tenure-eligible faculty members provide more or less adequate education to undergraduates than do tenured faculty.[14] We hear extensive claims of teaching effectiveness from both tenure-track and non-tenure-track faculty, but none of these is supported by convincing data. Without such information, how can we know whether hiring an additional person on the tenure track is the most appropriate way to address unmet undergraduate teaching needs?

Moreover, we train many of our PhD students, especially in the arts and sciences, for academic careers. Faculty advisers at elite universities measure their success as graduate teachers by the status of the placements that their graduate students achieve. Yet surveys count large numbers of PhDs who cannot find the kinds of jobs they want and who end up in lecturer or part-time academic roles. How can we justify the cost and time devoted to graduate education in certain fields without understanding the market for individuals with the training we provide?

University leaders talk endlessly about "teacher-scholars" who bring cutting-edge research to state-of-the-art teaching and who learn from teaching bright, challenging students who stimulate intellectual creativity and research productivity. As John Sexton, president of New York University warned, "To be attractive to students, the research university must ensure the connection between learning and research which is its justification."[15] Deans and provosts also stress the principles of academic freedom and "shared governance" and the essential role of faculty members in guiding our best institutions of higher learning, especially when it comes to curriculum, intellectual quality of students and faculty, and promising intellectual areas ripe for future development. At the same time, we are remarkably uninformed about the consequences for faculty makeup, faculty priorities, academic freedom, and faculty governance of hiring large numbers of teaching and research specialists who are not eligible for tenure. Is the day of the teacher-scholar coming to an end? Is academic freedom at serious risk? Will faculty governance continue to be able to operate on behalf of high-quality education *and* scholarship? These are some of the questions that drive our interest in understanding the forces that lead research universities to hire non-tenure-track faculty and the consequences of such hiring decisions for university functioning.

A great deal has been written about the increasing use of non-tenure-track faculty in the academy, most of it highly critical.[16] These writings assert that non-tenure-track faculty members are exploited and need to organize into unions: they teach too many courses, receive poor pay and poor (or no) benefits, are marginalized on campus, and often have to commute from campus to campus picking up piecework from multiple universities to put together full-time jobs with (barely) livable wages. These writings also assert that non-tenure-track instructors are unable to deliver high-quality education to undergraduates because they cannot spend the necessary time with their students, they lack private offices and even computers, and they have no opportunities for professional development. The premise of these writings is that the increasing use of lecturers is driven almost entirely by economics, that non-tenure-track faculty are unable to offer the same high-quality educational experiences to undergraduates as do tenure-track faculty, and that the continued practice of hiring non-tenure-track instructors will threaten academic freedom and the existence of the tenure system.[17]

Some of these claims are true in our nation's most elite universities; others are not. The many reasons for hiring non-tenure-track faculty to teach undergraduates rarely receive any attention at all. Painting a more complete and accurate picture of practices on these select campuses is one of our goals. To identify realistic possibilities for change, we also go beyond practices to explain why they exist and what kinds of consequences they produce.

Statistical studies of faculty hiring trends abound, but they cannot explain how or why individual employment decisions are made.[18] They overlook the fact that definitions are inconsistent as different universities apply different titles to the same instructional categories, and they blur important economic and geographical differences among colleges and universities. Many institutions do not have data systems that are adequate for understanding the non-tenure-track issue. Accurate data-management systems are relatively new on many campuses. In some cases, they are the product of one budget officer's efforts rather than any broader institutional initiative. This means that different institutions vary in the lengths of their historical records and that different categories of instructor are often not effectively differentiated. For example, many institutions have data systems that do not distinguish graduate student teaching assistants from part-time instructors.[19]

This data deficiency is often compounded when busy academic administrators restrict their attention to high-profile tenured faculty. Although most administrators know how many tenure-track faculty are employed at their institution (and how many full-time equivalents, or FTEs, they represent), they are much less aware of the numbers of non-tenure-track instructors. The answer to the question "How many tenure-track faculty positions do you have?" is typically precise (for example, "324"), but the answer to the question "How many non-tenure-track faculty do you have?" is often vague ("I think it is about 20 percent"). Worse, different officers of the same institution often come up with very different percentage estimates. Unless the non-tenure-track faculty are organized by a union and have a negotiated contract, university leaders are also poorly informed about the conditions of employment of their teaching specialists. Salaries, fractions, and duties may be arranged department by department, with little central oversight.

Therefore, we needed a different approach. After developing summary profiles of our ten institutions, we visited each campus. Our goals for these visits were threefold. First, we sought disaggregated institutional data on the instructional mix (tenure-track, graduate teaching assistants, non-tenure-track faculty) in arts and sciences and in engineering, over time. To the greatest extent possible, we sought detailed data that would permit distinctions across disciplines and levels of instruction. These data generally came from the institutional support personnel who create and maintain university or college data systems. We supplemented these data with extensive discussions with a wide range of academic administrators (including presidents, provosts, deans of schools and colleges, department chairs, and faculty members) to learn about their hiring and budget processes and about the reasons why their universities employ instructors off the tenure track. We explored actual and potential consequences, including unionization efforts, faculty morale, and governance problems. We explored how the systems of faculty appointments work, how various instructional needs are met (and why), what special problems are addressed by employing non-tenure-track faculty, and whether the numbers of non-tenure-track faculty create problems that are recognized by the university leaders themselves.[20]

Our campus visits proved invaluable. We benefitted tremendously from the interpretations of knowledgeable insiders. They enabled us to go beyond simple descriptions to paint a more complete picture of the educational commitments of elite research universities. They helped us understand the forces at work today that drive their undergraduate teaching missions and the consequences of today's hiring practices for quality education and healthy academic environments.

We start in the next chapter with a description of trends in the use of non-tenure-track faculty in arts and sciences and in engineering in our ten elite universities. Despite primitive management information systems, we see a general picture of growth in numbers over time that mirrors the reports in other studies. In subsequent chapters, we turn to each of four realities that complicate the lives of university leaders who might try to stem this growth—frequent presidential turnover, competition among universities, decentralized decision making, and budgetary reforms based on business models.

Then we turn to five implications of growing specialization in faculty roles:

• First, non-tenure-track faculty members are forming unions, to the dismay of tenured faculty and administrators who view the academic enterprise as a mutually supportive intellectual and collegial community. Higher education is among the few growth sectors for organized labor today for both teaching assistants and instructors off the tenure track.

- Second, over time, non-tenure-track faculty members are teaching an increasing percentage of credit hours that are offered to undergraduates, but we know remarkably little about what that means for the quality of the educational experiences that our students have. We describe some of the existing data and explain their limitations in answering this fundamental question.

- Third, tenure-track faculty members are deeply involved in graduate education. Their own reputations depend in part on how successfully they place their PhD students, and non-tenure-track positions are not regarded as successes. Yet these same faculty members sometimes avoid undergraduate teaching, thereby encouraging more non-tenure-track hiring to cover undergraduate courses.

- Fourth, insufficient attention to governance issues in an environment with large numbers of teaching and research specialists may compromise the effectiveness of academic decision making and lead to unanticipated and negative consequences for the health of the academic enterprise.

- Fifth, the growth of non-tenure-track faculty numbers constitutes an erosion of the tenure system. There is remarkably little attention to this—and to possible erosion in academic freedom—by the tenured faculty on our nation's elite campuses today.

Finally, we describe several critical dilemmas facing university leaders that have an impact on the makeup of their campus workforce, and we offer some advice for dealing with them effectively.

2

Setting the Stage: The Changing Complexion of Postsecondary Instruction

Consider the romance of higher education—the university as a collection of brick and white-painted buildings in an idyllic setting (preferably in New England) populated by well-meaning if slightly absent-minded instructors wearing rumpled clothing who are committed to the intellectual growth of their students, to the insights and intricacies of their disciplinary specialties, and to the health of their own institutions. That such a nostalgic image may never have reflected reality does not diminish the fact that it has been more or less accepted (even by many faculty members themselves) as an apt description of life in higher education.

Tenure is not an essential part of this image, for no one would challenge the integrity or the employment security of well-meaning people who are willing to work for modest pay in an essentially unglamorous profession. Nonetheless, tenure has become an important and contested feature of faculty life. Faculty and faculty organizations protect tenure as a defense of academic freedom—a bulwark against the attempts of university administrators, donors, governing board members, the media, and elected public officials to stifle the expression of unpopular opinions or criticism of those in power. On the other hand, public views of tenure can be harsh. To the public and even to university administrators, tenure can sometimes be seen as indefinite job security that can provide unwarranted protection to superfluous, lazy, incompetent, or even subversive individuals who ought to be dismissed (as they would from any private-sector enterprise).

Neither of these descriptions—tenure as defense or tenure as job security—captures the full significance of tenure in higher education. Many nontenured employees in universities spend their entire careers in

their positions. Their teaching contributions are valued by their colleagues—tenured and untenured alike—and their termination would
never be seriously considered. Even their vulnerability to termination is
doubtful. As university employers know, labor legislation in many states
prohibits capricious dismissal of long-term employees, even if the employment term is composed of a long series of one-year contracts. One of
our most knowledgeable interviewees commented, "For all intents and
purposes, general faculty (those without tenure) are tenured. It's hard to
let them go. If you have been reappointed twice, you have the expectation of continuing employment." The provost at this same institution
noted that general faculty members have access to faculty grievance
procedures, and a dean commented: "We've never tried to get rid of
general faculty members. To get rid of them, we'd have to eliminate the
entire program. It would be very hard."

Nevertheless, elite research universities reserve tenure for faculty
members who excel in research. Setting a very high bar for scholarship
in tenure decisions is what maintains the outstanding scholarly reputations of these universities, and many faculty members describe tenure
decisions as the most important decisions they make. In the tenure
process, decision makers review each case and try to make an educated
forecast of the likelihood of continued excellence and future international stature at the very top of the person's field of study. The best
indicators are the quality of past work, the proposals for future work,
the judgments of outside experts at the top of the field, the success in
raising research funds (in some fields) from respected sources that rely
on peer review, and the recognition that comes with major national and
international prizes and recognitions.

Everyone involved in this process knows that the stakes are high. The
number of tenured slots is limited, and there is a powerful incentive to
avoid mistakes—that is, promotions that award tenure to individuals
who will never produce scholarship of the highest caliber. Everyone recognizes that the granting of tenure is a multimillion-dollar commitment
by the university and that those who do not produce will probably stay
for their entire careers—which could be long now that there is no
required retirement age. For universities vying for continued placement
at the very top, every decision matters. This perspective on the awarding

of tenure has made the advancement of proposals to provide tenure to teaching specialists very difficult on research campuses. Every promotion committee views a positive tenure decision as locking up a position that potentially could be occupied by a Nobel Prize laureate.

Determining who should and who should not be tenured occupies a great deal of time and effort by faculty and administrators on our nation's campuses. Therefore, we find it surprising that so few faculty members understand what tenure actually means, in general and on their specific campuses. We suspect that few have ever read the American Association of University Professors (AAUP) statement on academic tenure, the first paragraph of which reads, "After the expiration of a probationary period, teachers or investigators should have permanent or continuous tenure, and their service should be terminated only for adequate cause, except in the case of retirement for age, or under extraordinary circumstances because of financial exigencies."[1] The AAUP statement then goes on to describe the process by which "adequate cause" might be established and employment lost.

Today, chairs and deans try hard to educate faculty about the procedures for tenure reviews but devote little attention to the procedures that are available to tenured faculty to appeal negative rulings on salary, continued employment, and so forth. On the campuses in our study, few occasions prompt grievances by tenured faculty members, and education takes place infrequently and sporadically when those events occur.

In practical terms, *holding tenure* means that a faculty member who is threatened with termination (or other adverse action) has access to a protracted and tedious grievance procedure that can be followed by several steps of appeal. At least one step in this process consists of a review by a faculty committee. This is an essential ingredient: whatever actions the university administration wishes to take are subject to faculty review if they are appealed. At some (but not all) universities, administrators retain authority to take action anyway, even in the face of faculty criticism, but the cost of doing so is high in terms of the administrator's and the institution's reputation. Presidents, provosts, and deans on elite research campuses are loath to ignore faculty opinion and are therefore unlikely to overrule a faculty committee's recommendation on an appeal. This reality makes job security for tenured faculty a matter of academic culture rather than of contract. If it should happen that various administrative levels and the faculty at large should agree that termination is appropriate, then there is nothing (apart from civil employment law or other external intervention) to prevent it.

What is unclear is the extent to which that same academic culture offers protection to individuals who do *not* hold tenure. It clearly retains some bite. Dismissal of a faculty member, tenured or not, is sufficiently rare to be newsworthy. When it occurs for reasons seen to be related to classroom content or political outlook, almost all faculty regard it as a fundamental challenge to academic values and to the principle that the classroom is sacrosanct. Tenured faculty may be much more protective of their tenured colleagues than they are of untenured faculty, but they regard the open discussion of issues from all perspectives, whether controversial or not, as the proper business of a college or university. In the end, this value system provides significant job protection for all faculty members, tenured or not. If that value system were to disappear (as it has in some religious colleges and in the for-profit sector), the benefits of tenure would disappear along with it.[2]

One consequential practice of tenured faculty in our nation's prestigious research universities is that they exert considerable authority over the selection of the courses they teach. Typically, untenured faculty members have their teaching duties assigned to them. Once the tenured faculty have chosen their courses, the department chair identifies remaining course needs each year and appoints lecturers, visitors, or adjunct faculty members to meet them. Acceptance of those specific course assignments is a condition of employment. A non-tenure-track faculty member who refuses such an assignment, on whatever grounds, provides a compelling reason for nonreappointment or dismissal, and labor law and faculty values provide no protection.

A tenured faculty member, on the other hand, can refuse an assignment with near impunity at an elite research university. Department chairs certainly have influence (especially if they have a role in salary determination), and collegial values do operate. Groups of faculty in a discipline or subdiscipline discuss teaching assignments among themselves, but the spirit is one of coordination rather than mandate. An important reality is that tenured faculty members at elite universities typically are given the courses, graduate or undergraduate, that they would most like to teach, leaving the remainder of the curriculum to the untenured faculty and graduate students.

This often happens without meaningful administrative oversight. At one of the universities we visited, a major department refused to provide the provost with detailed information about who was teaching each of its courses, and the provost was reluctant to insist. At another, a course that was required for completing a PhD program had not been offered for several years because tenured faculty were unwilling to teach it.

Tenured faculty at elite universities, unlike those at liberal arts colleges, take research leaves whenever they can finance them, sometimes leaving entire portions of the curriculum in need of teaching replacements for the year. They also choose when they want to teach, leaving the less desirable teaching times to untenured colleagues, without much regard for choosing times thought to be most effective pedagogically. Efforts to use classrooms more efficiently—especially on Fridays, in the early mornings, and in the evenings—are difficult to implement in part because tenured faculty have strong preferences for other teaching times.[3]

Tenure also provides an important status and economic symbol. A tenure review can be an ordeal, and surviving the tenure process at an elite university is a sign of recognition by one's peers of the quality of one's scholarship. Individuals in non-tenure-track positions are rarely first-rank scholars, and they are not likely to pass a difficult tenure review should they go through one.

In salary terms, modern colleges and universities still adhere to a relatively egalitarian value system. As the research hierarchy gains more and more force, this egalitarianism is beginning to crumble, but a strong sense still exists that persons with the same title in the same department should carry roughly the same compensation. For example, when salaries for some full professors fall below those of associate professors in the same department or when salaries of associates are below those of assistants, chairs argue for "equity adjustments" to correct what are seen as inappropriate inversions in compensation. Egalitarianism does not cross departmental or college lines, however, leaving salaries of professors in many humanities fields below those of associate professors or even assistant professors in social science and science departments. Egalitarianism also does not cross tenure boundaries, making it easy for universities to set vastly different compensation levels for tenured and nontenured faculty, even within the same department.[4]

Despite some progress in recent years, tenure is also associated with gender. Women are still underrepresented in tenured positions in many fields, especially at the full professor level, and they are *over*represented in non-tenure-track teaching positions. Women are also less likely than men to move from non-tenure-track to tenure-track status. As Schuster and Finkelstein report,

Academic women, despite their infusion into the academy in large numbers, suffer in comparison to men in the types of academic appointments they hold. . . . women are twice as likely as the men to be found in non-tenure-eligible positions. . . . The proportion of women who are tenured has also continued at much lower rates than for men.[5]

Views of tenure are strongly held by those on and off campus, but they are rapidly losing their relevance as we chronicle the progression of hiring in higher education. No one can ignore the rapid growth in the use of faculty without tenure, often without full-time positions, without long-term employment guarantees, and without the status accorded to the traditional full-time tenured faculty. While tenured faculty would undoubtedly rise up in protest against any proposal to eliminate tenure, those on elite research campuses are remarkably silent about the steady expansion of the nontenure role in the academy.[6]

Growing Numbers of Non-Tenure-Track Faculty: But How Many Are There?

Faculty members in non-tenure-eligible positions are now employed by every major university in America. They teach, advise students, coordinate graduate student teaching (and teacher training), in rare cases chair departments, and perform many other critical services that keep universities functioning. They also conduct research, although doing so is not generally a condition of their employment. Their presence on campus is not new. They show up consistently in university appointment data from the 1970s and even earlier,[7] but their recent growth in numbers has been remarkable.[8]

The use of non-tenure-track faculty is much more common outside the orbit of the elite research universities that provide the focus of our study. Expansion of the for-profit sector of higher education is supported almost entirely by instruction without tenure, and many two-year institutions similarly rely heavily on non-tenure-track faculty. What is surprising is the significant growth in the numbers of non-tenure-track faculty even in the most elite of our universities.

Given the countless reports and publications that describe (and often decry) the rising numbers of non-tenure-track faculty, one might assume that tracking their numbers over time would be easy. That is emphatically *not* the case. Identifying exactly who falls under the category of non-tenure-track faculty turns out to be surprisingly complicated. We have defined *non-tenure-track (NTT) faculty* to be those university employees who, although not eligible for tenure review, nevertheless perform teaching duties. Under this definition, in addition to those who are commonly called *lecturers* or *adjuncts*, NTT faculty include a number of staff members who teach occasionally but who do not have teaching as their primary responsibility—administrators, postdoctoral fellows, research scientists, extension faculty, visiting faculty, academic advisors, and emeritus faculty who continue to teach. The definition encompasses both full-time and part-time appointments. It does not include *graduate student instructors* or *assistants (GSIs or GSTAs)*, or other students of the institution whose teaching, research, or advising service is part of their degree training.[9]

Available institutional data do not always track our definition or, indeed, any consistent and meaningful definition that we could discover. The distinction between graduate student teaching and teaching by NTT faculty is frequently blurred. The distinctions among long-term lecturers, part-time adjuncts, and academic visitors who hold tenure elsewhere were also unclear on many campuses. Most campuses have no reliable data on teaching activity by research scientists or emeriti faculty. No single definition removes ambiguities of this sort, and that difficulty is reflected in university data systems, most of which also appear unable to categorize instructional types consistently.

When we cast our net widely for those who teach courses at major research institutions, we find a large and diverse group of employees.

Universities do not consider this large group in its entirety. Definitions of tenure-track faculty are relatively clear: the terms *full, associate* (sometimes *with* and sometimes *without tenure)*, and (in most cases) *assistant professor* have common meanings across academe. In contrast, NTT positions are categorized and labeled differently at virtually every institution. Even the term *non-tenure-track faculty*, which we use throughout this work, is not standard: NTT faculty are variously referred to in higher-education articles and other studies as "contract faculty,"[10] "contingent faculty,"[11] "part-time faculty"[12] (misleading because many full-time faculty nevertheless still have no opportunity for tenure review), "term-limited faculty"[13] (misleading because many NTT faculty spend their entire careers at one institution), "professors of practice,"[14] and "adjunct faculty."[15]

Below is a partial list of the titles and categories that are used to describe non-tenure-track faculty in at least one of the ten institutions we visited:

- Adjunct professors
- Visiting professors
- Emeritus professors (when they teach courses)
- Recalled retirees
- Postdocs (when they teach courses)
- Lecturers (including lecturers 1, 2, 3, and 4)
- Senior lecturers
- College lecturers
- Lecturers with the expectation of continuing employment or security of employment
- Instructors (often teaching coordinators)
- Teaching associates
- Technical instructors
- General faculty
- Academic professionals
- Professors of the practice
- Faculty without tenure (WOT) by reason of funding

• Research faculty (when they teach courses)
• Research scientists (when they teach courses)
• Recalled faculty
• Acting faculty
• Assistant professors (postdocs who sometimes are facetiously known as occupying "folding chairs")

This bewildering array of job titles leads to confusion even across a single campus. We heard faculty members and administrators using titles to describe non-tenure-track faculty positions that were different from those used by institutional researchers at the same university. At one major public university, for example, deans and department chairs consistently referred to all NTT faculty as "academic professionals." Yet as the senior institutional researcher later informed us, most NTT faculty are lecturers and definitely *not* academic professionals; lecturers on that campus are not eligible for the one-year "notice rights" available to all academic professionals. At another large urban public university, the title "instructor" appeared occasionally in appointment data, but the institutional researcher himself did not know how this job title might differ from the more common "lecturer" or why it was listed as a separate type of position. At a third, NTT faculty members were called "general faculty," and their titles could parallel those of the regular faculty—such as "associate professor of the general faculty." As a consequence, outsiders find it difficult to tell from job titles whether these individuals are eligible for tenure. An institutional data expert on that campus offered his views of how job titles are assigned: "When departments hire NTT people, they can throw any title at them they want. . . . I can't find any consistent way to figure out who they are, so I don't include them in my tables [which he prepares for the president]." Later he said, "The Colleges of Engineering and Arts and Sciences have their own separate data systems. Sometimes my data differs from theirs by quite a lot."

On several of our campuses, research scientists are now called *research professors*. They may have certain employment guarantees, they may serve on PhD dissertation committees, they may teach an occasional course, and they sometimes have full voting rights in departmental hiring and promotion decisions. Outsiders would be hard-pressed to know whether the research professor title means a distinguished teacher-scholar with tenure or a research-only member of the university staff. In sum, several of the universities we visited had no standard titles or policies for NTT faculty, and those that did had standardized their titles and policies only recently. Confusion and regular misuse of job titles remains common. One of our public universities was in the process of developing an eighteen-category classification system for instructors to respond to persistent legislative inquiries about teaching. None of the people we interviewed was convinced that this system could be implemented successfully.

Among the most problematic titles is that of "assistant professor." In some settings, postdoctoral instructors are given this title, even though they are not eligible for tenure review and will have to leave after the traditional probationary period has expired. In other settings, assistant professors are eligible for tenure review, but the number of available tenured slots is so much smaller than the number of eligible assistant professors that most necessarily fail in their tenure reviews. After the fact, they will be indistinguishable from non-tenure-track faculty. Such cases would never be included in the numbers of NTT faculty, but their odds of achieving tenure at a few very selective private institutions are so small that their colleagues treat them like NTT faculty.

Not coincidentally, we found that most universities and the colleges and schools within them do a poor job of tracking their own NTT faculty. Even those staff specifically charged with the maintenance of institutional data are unable to respond to basic questions about the number of NTT faculty employed, in which departments, how long NTT faculty have been at the university, what their duties are, and what their average salaries and benefits packages are—statistics that are readily available for the regular tenure-line faculty. Institutional researchers commonly speak of the heroic efforts required to assemble these kinds of data in one place.

 No university in our study was able to provide student-oriented teaching data by faculty type—that is, how many students are taught in classes led by tenure-track faculty, non-tenure-track faculty, and graduate

<u>students.</u> The reason is that universities usually maintain teaching assignment data in the offices of associate deans or department chairs, while personnel data, including tenure status, are maintained elsewhere. Graduate student appointments are usually stored in a third dataset. The software databases themselves are frequently incompatible, so that even if universities were inclined to merge all of this information into one whole, the technical barriers would be nearly insurmountable. One data expert commented, "We would have to merge human resources data with the student data to find out what individual instructors are teaching. I've never been really confident about the accuracy of the student system with respect to who's teaching what. In some departments, the faculty instructor will be listed for all the labs or sections, and in others, the TAs themselves will be listed." Another said, "We really need a database that allows us to track students better. If you find out exactly how many students are in the Grad School of Arts and Sciences, let me know." A graduate dean said that "people ask me all the time how many graduate students we have at. . . . I don't know."

It may be surprising that our nation's prestigious institutions have such primitive management information systems. After all, these same universities are world leaders in information technology in support of research. Their faculty members regularly maintain enormous databases of social, economic, and biological data. Their science faculty download, transmit, and analyze massive flows of experimental data. Faculty in certain humanities areas maintain computer programs that analyze and summarize complex linguistic data. And yet these same institutions are unable to define and count their own instructional staff or graduate student body. Worse, they respond regularly to national employment surveys from the U.S. Department of Education, legislative bodies, accrediting agencies, the AAUP, and numerous others, and those agencies in turn publish those data aggregated and disaggregated in ways that presume that categories are reliably defined. Once those numbers are published in formal tables, they acquire an appearance of precision—but it is a fictitious precision that is in no way reflected in the information systems available at the source.

Institutional researchers may be incompletely informed about numbers of non-tenure-track faculty on their campuses, but top academic administrators (presidents, provosts, and deans) are even less well informed. Particularly in settings in which a number of different titles are applied to NTT faculty, university leaders tend to underestimate the number who are employed in their own organizations. In most cases, they are also poorly informed about the conditions of employment of NTT faculty—their pay, benefits, work assignments, work environments—unless complaints come forward or unions become active. For example, one frustrated dean of engineering said that he had no working information system at all and could not answer even basic questions about his faculty. Several arts and sciences deans told us they had no faculty data before 1990, and another began collecting college data in 1995 in response to a direct request from the president. Even then, the data focused only on tenured and tenure-track faculty.

As a consequence, developing a common database about NTT faculty to facilitate comparisons across institutions is a significant challenge. There are no common classifications and reporting standards in use for NTT faculty as there are for faculty subject to tenure review. Time-series data describing NTT faculty are either difficult to gather or simply non-existent, and schools or colleges within the institutions provide data of widely divergent quality and scope. Given this reality, we have come to believe that national data assembled from either university reports or surveys seriously understate the presence of NTT faculty on campuses as a whole.

Even the NTT faculty themselves are often unclear about their status. National surveys that seek self-identification of NTT faculty do not receive responses from academic administrators or emeritus faculty who also teach occasional courses, from research faculty who teach, or from well-compensated professionals who teach occasionally as adjuncts. Although members of all these groups are without tenure and in principle could be terminated at will by their employers, few see themselves in this light, and few are likely to respond to surveys inquiring about their working conditions.

We draw inferences from what we learned from our interviews on ten campuses. We provide supporting empirical evidence in basic areas, but the bulk of what we know comes from firsthand encounters with the decision makers themselves and not from what they are able to report in electronic files.

Who Teaches Undergraduates, and How Has This Changed over Time?

Most of our ten institutions were able to provide some information about who teaches undergraduates in arts and sciences and engineering, by type of appointment, although they vary in terms of how long they have been collecting such information. Even from these limited data, it is clear that much of the growth in NTT numbers has occurred in introductory courses, especially in foreign language and composition courses.

We focus on arts and sciences and engineering colleges (or their equivalents) at each institution because they include most of the departments that have traditionally been responsible for teaching "core" courses, and they typically teach most of the undergraduates on campus. We start by asking how much of the undergraduate teaching responsibility is borne by instructors off the tenure track or graduate students or regular faculty in tenure lines and how that has been changing over time.

Arts and Sciences Colleges

Eight of the institutions in our study were able to provide time series that shed some light on the question of growth in non-tenure-track faculty numbers in arts and sciences. The data are not comparable across institutions, partly because of differences in definition and partly because the types of data gathered were different. For example, in half of the cases, the data refer to headcounts (the numbers of people in the category regardless of their part-time or full-time status) rather than full-time equivalents (FTE) because that was what was available. Available time series are usually very short, reflecting the fact that supporting data-collection efforts were only recently established. In one case, the university changed its management information system in a way that ended comparability between current and historical data series. In the missing two cases, either the data were unavailable, or the definitions of NTT faculty had been changed in a way that precluded the construction of a consistent series. The data that we do have from arts and sciences colleges are presented in the appendix to this chapter.

Some NTT faculty members hold part-time positions, so we expect headcounts to be larger than FTE totals. Only one of our institutions provided data of both types. Comparing the two types of data in that single case, one headcount unit of NTT faculty was approximately equivalent to .83 units of FTE faculty. That is, the average NTT faculty member is working 83 percent time. Regardless of whether we look at headcounts or FTEs, we do see a growth in the relative use of NTT faculty in general at an annual rate of about 3.1 percent per year since 1990—which would accumulate to an increase of almost 36 percent over a decade.[16] Putting this in the perspective of actual data values, this means that an average arts and sciences college (at an elite research university) that employed 150 FTE of NTT faculty in 1995 would have increased that contingent to 204 FTE of NTT faculty by 2005. Meanwhile, the number of tenure-track faculty in arts and sciences has remained roughly constant.

Given that NTT faculty offer more courses per year on average than TT faculty and that their teaching is usually concentrated in the first two years of the undergraduate programs, the percentage of first- and second-year undergraduate credit hours taught by NTT faculty has increased substantially. Averaging across the eight institutions for which we have consistent data, it appears that, in lower-division arts and sciences courses, NTT faculty teach approximately the same number of credit hours as TT faculty (although the deviations above and below this mean can be significant). Moreover, these numbers do not reflect the undergraduate teaching by graduate students, which also is predominantly in the lower division. Today, tenure-track faculty are teaching significantly fewer than half of all the credit hours generated in the lower division in arts and sciences in many of our nation's most prestigious universities. We have here some confirmation of the widely held suspicion that while the reputations and rankings of these institutions are based largely on the distinction of tenured faculty members, these individuals infrequently come in contact with first- or second-year college students. Most leaders of research universities are concerned about the need to include first- and second-year courses in the teaching responsibilities of their most distinguished faculty and have taken steps to encourage that. None, however, acknowledge publicly that their presence is as small as it is today.[17]

Engineering Colleges

NTT faculty appointments have increased in engineering, as well, but less rapidly than they have increased in arts and sciences. The growth in numbers of tenure-track faculty in engineering has proceeded at almost the same rate, so that the proportion of NTT faculty relative to TT faculty has been almost constant over the last decade in engineering schools. At the same time, these numbers understate the growing importance of NTT faculty in engineering education for three reasons. First, much of the teaching of fundamentals for engineering students (mathematics, physics, chemistry, and writing) is done in arts and sciences colleges in the very courses that make greatest use of NTT faculty. That is, the appearance of lesser use of NTT faculty in engineering colleges arises from the fact that they are not appointing the NTT faculty themselves but are using NTT faculty members who are appointed elsewhere.

Second, the growth in engineering TT faculty has been fueled by a growth in funded research volume. This expansion does not produce equivalent growth in full-time teaching but in numbers of faculty who spend significant parts of their time on research. In this case, an FTE of TT faculty does not mean an FTE of teaching effort. Sophisticated data-management techniques would capture this distinction by quantifying teaching effort, thus enabling us to compare the teaching efforts of NTT and TT faculty, but such detail is not generated routinely. It could be generated as a management research effort, but we did not find any active efforts along those lines.

Third, this same growth in research volume has led to a rapid increase in the numbers of research scientists in engineering colleges. Although these individuals sometimes participate in instruction (especially during gaps in external funding), university data systems rarely include them in their NTT datasets even when they do teach.

Which Departments Use Non-Tenure-Track Faculty?

As expected, within arts and sciences colleges, the largest numbers of non-tenure-track faculty are concentrated in departments with large lower-division undergraduate teaching needs—English, mathematics, economics, Spanish, and writing and composition. English departments stand out for their heavy use of NTT faculty for undergraduate writing instruction. The need for introductory writing courses is great because they are required for virtually all students, but they are taught most effectively in small sections. This leads to a large demand for instructors. At the same time, research universities are reluctant to expand their English Department faculty by enough to cover these courses, especially since many tenure-track faculty in language and literature departments are unenthusiastic about teaching writing. The result is a heavy reliance on NTT faculty to teach composition. The same could be said about teaching elementary Spanish.[18]

While the largest numbers of NTT faculty in arts and sciences are still in the humanities, similar pressures exist in other areas of the curriculum, and most of the liberal arts disciplines have experienced growth in non-tenure-track faculty over the past two decades.[19] In mathematics, for example, the teaching capacity of the regular faculty is often too small even to teach the number of calculus sections offered on campus—much less the rest of the curriculum. TT faculty are supplemented (or replaced) by graduate teaching assistants, postdocs, or lecturers. With fellowship dollars available for graduate students, one of our math departments used forty or more postdocs each year to teach calculus sections. Another math department hired local junior college faculty to offer a number of courses as overloads. Many math departments that do rely on TT faculty teach calculus in large lecture formats that require fewer faculty resources, even though learning may be more effective in small classes. Similar issues arise in introductory science courses and laboratories in biology and chemistry. The growth of lower-division teaching needs in these areas is often met by NTT faculty, graduate students, and, in some cases, even upper-level undergraduate majors who tutor or grade.

A few universities sought to limit the growth in NTT faculty by limiting the demand for introductory courses. One of the institutions in our study requires only one year of a foreign language and accepts high school credits to satisfy that, a move designed to reduce the need for NTT faculty in Spanish. A few others export certain subjects to local community colleges (especially foreign language and introductory composition) by creating understandings about transfer credits and accepting large numbers of transfer students. In effect, the number of NTT faculty at such an institution can be held down by a strategy of exporting the instruction to faculty who are employed somewhere else. Others sought to slow or reverse the increases by raising the funds to replace NTT faculty with tenure-stream faculty, but that is an expensive proposition, as we discuss below.

Why Hire Non-Tenure-Track Faculty?

The growth in non-tenure-track faculty at elite research universities is not always the result of conscious policy but instead often emerges as a by-product of other initiatives. One of the reasons for the relative invisibility of the NTT instructional faculty to university administrators may be that the original reasons for hiring them are not economic or even teaching related. Here is a typical example of the kind of process that is at work. As the job market for PhD graduates in English began to weaken in the 1980s, professors became increasingly concerned that their own graduates would not be successful in finding academic employment. In an effort to strengthen their credentials, departments created programs that would retain their own graduates in one-year NTT positions. The purpose was the laudable one of giving PhD graduates time to further their research and to gain teaching experience to make them more attractive to prospective employers. Unfortunately, the strategy was not always immediately successful, and pressures grew to extend the program for an additional year to support those still seeking positions. The one-year appointment was renewed for a second year, then for a third, and so on, until at last, programs of temporary support for graduate students had metamorphosed into support for a cadre of semipermanent NTT English instructors holding PhDs from their own institution. Occasionally, their numbers approached or even exceeded the number of TT faculty who had originally trained them![20]

A second example can be seen in instruction in specialized, highly compensated disciplines. Faculty who teach constitutional law or law and society can make higher salaries teaching in law schools than in arts and sciences; faculty who teach economics are recruited by business schools that pay better than arts and sciences; and faculty who teach medical history or ethics can find more lucrative assignments in medical schools. Liberal arts colleges that hire tenured faculty to teach in these areas have great difficulty keeping them in the face of offers from professional schools. In the interim, colleges may turn to adjunct (NTT) faculty to meet instructional needs. Sometimes departments experience one loss after another, and the interim becomes semipermanent.

Much has been made of the cost savings that result from hiring NTT rather than TT faculty. Indeed, most of the literature suggests that the growth of NTT faculty has been driven by deliberate university or college efforts to replace expensive TT faculty with less expensive teaching talent. There is no doubt that heightened national and international competition for TT faculty has led to higher salaries for some, higher set-up costs, dual-career employment requirements, housing subsidies, and lower teaching loads, and these all have driven up the costs per TT faculty member and per course taught by TT faculty. Most university budgets have not increased nearly as rapidly, particularly in public universities.

One can see just how expensive it is to hire additional tenure-track faculty by looking at two of our universities that announced plans to add tenure-track faculty. The University of Virginia announced a ten-year plan to add 300 tenure-track faculty members at an estimated cost of $130,000 each.[21] The University of Michigan announced a five-year plan to add 100 junior faculty at a cost of more than $100,000 each in salary and benefits plus more than $20 million in one-time start-up and renovation costs.[22]

Despite the plausibility of the budget motive for hiring NTT rather than TT faculty, the process is much more subtle than that. Budget stringency certainly supports the growth of NTT faculty positions, but as in the just cited case of the English departments, it may not be the initial driver. Indeed, if cost were the only factor, we would not see dramatic differences in the use of NTT faculty across departments within the same institution. We would especially not expect more NTT faculty in humanities departments, where salaries, equipment, and laboratory costs for TT faculty are much lower than they are in the sciences. Interviews with provosts, deans, and chairs at our various universities revealed a number of drivers besides cost that have led them to hire NTT faculty:

• The use of adjuncts who bring special knowledge and experience into the academy (for example, creative writers and computer animation experts),

• The offering of continued teaching opportunities to older faculty as a retirement inducement necessitated by the termination of mandatory retirement,

• The wish to support long-term research faculty whose research funding has temporarily lapsed,

• The need to replace faculty temporarily on leave,

• The need to expand offerings in response to surges in enrollment that are thought to be temporary,

• Resistance on the part of tenured faculty to teach certain courses (especially beginning language courses, introductory composition, calculus, and laboratory coordination) and to fill certain roles in advising and curriculum coordination,

• The need to teach courses in fields where recruitment and retention are difficult (such as public law, actuarial science, and economics),

• The decision to offer courses in new fields (such as Korean studies or comparative media studies) where the pool of well-trained PhDs still needs development,

• The expanding need for remedial education or for intensive education that requires more classroom hours of instruction than the market for tenure-track faculty will support, and

• New budgeting systems that create incentives to hire low-cost labor, increase enrollments, and capture tuition credit.

Additional motives that affect who teaches undergraduate courses derive from a concern about supporting and strengthening graduate education:

• The integration of teacher training and experience into graduate teaching programs,

• The reliance on teaching as a means of financial support for graduate students, and

• The growing use of "teaching postdocs" as a way of preparing new PhDs for teaching careers (and a way of bringing young talent to campus for future recruitment).

These motives have to do with much more than cost, and many of them are designed to make improvements in higher education. They concern improving programs, maintaining flexibility in light of future uncertainty of enrollment patterns, encouraging research grants and outside faculty fellowships, coping with the end of mandatory retirement, responding to demographic changes in the undergraduate population and insufficient preparation in high schools, growing careerism of students and parents, and increasing competition for tenured faculty. In the next chapter, we describe how academic hiring decisions are actually made and by whom.

Appendix 2A

The two figures in this appendix represent the pattern of non-tenure-track employment in arts and sciences for the eight universities that were able to provide us with internally consistent data. The data are not comparable across institutions, partly because of differences in definition and partly because the types of data gathered were different. The trend lines in figure 2.1 represent headcounts, and the lines in figure 2.2 represent full-time equivalents. The numbers of NTT faculty have likely been underestimated because universities fail to count many who fall into the NTT category. The short lines in several cases reflect the recency of collection efforts. In one case, the university changed its management information system in a way that ended comparability between current and historical data series (hence an early end point). In the missing two

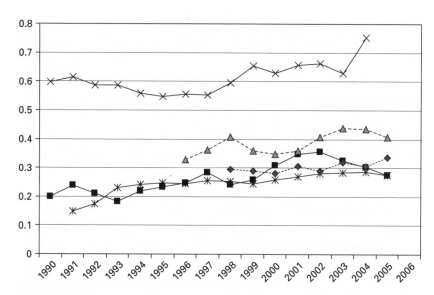

Figure 2.1
Ratio of non-tenure-track faculty to tenure-track faculty head count

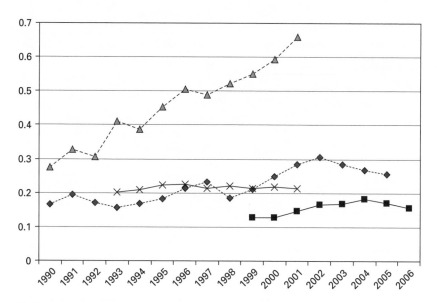

Figure 2.2
Ratio of non-tenure-track faculty to tenure-track full-time equivalents

legend ?!

cases, either the data were unavailable, or the definitions of NTT faculty had been changed so substantially that no meaningful series could be presented.

Even granting the deficiencies in the data, it is clear that, overall, the use of NTT faculty in arts and sciences on these elite campuses has been growing over the last decade, just as the national data suggest. This growth contrasts with the fact that tenure-track numbers in arts and sciences have remained flat or even fallen modestly. With this in mind, we constructed graphs that describe the *ratio* of NTT faculty to TT faculty.

We had expected the use of NTT faculty to be lower in private universities than in the publics, in part because the private institutions in our sample are generally well-endowed and in part because the large undergraduate enrollments in public institutions present special challenges to high-quality undergraduate education. Our data do not support that expectation, although we are not prepared to come to any firm conclusion: sample sizes are small, and the variability within each sample type is large.

Figure 2.1 presents the ratio charts for the five institutions in our sample that were able to provide consistent headcount data for arts and sciences faculty over time. Figure 2.2 presents the ratio charts for the four institutions in our sample that were able to provide consistent full-time equivalent data for arts and sciences faculty over time.

3

How Are Academic Hiring Decisions Made?

And now I come to a peculiar characteristic of our administrative apparatus. . . .
When an affair has been weighed for a very long time, it may happen, even before
the matter has been fully considered, that suddenly in a flash the decision comes
in some unforeseen place, which, moreover, can't be found any longer later on—
a decision that settles the matter, if in most cases justly, yet all the same arbitrarily.
It's as if the administrative apparatus were unable any longer to bear the tension,
the year-long irritation caused by the same affair—probably trivial in itself—and
had hit on the decision by itself, without the assistance of the officials. Of course,
a miracle didn't happen and certainly it was some clerk who hit upon the solu-
tion or the unwritten decision, but in any case it couldn't be discovered by us at
least, by us here, or even by the head bureau, which clerk had decided in this
case and on what grounds.

—Franz Kafka, *The Castle*[1]

We are certainly not the first to puzzle over how academic policies evolve
or struggle to identify the individuals who ultimately decide on resource
allocations in the modern university. Kafka had an important insight. It
is not that the decisions are necessarily wrong. Universities, after all, are
populated by intelligent and well-meaning people. It is that many outcomes seem to be generated more from amalgams of individual decisions
made deep within the infrastructure than from reasoned direction
from above.

Far from being intentional strategic behavior driven by university
boards, presidents, provosts, or deans, decisions to hire non-tenure-track
(NTT) instructors are usually made in departments, and the forces that
promote NTT hiring in elite research universities are much more subtle
than direct orders from the top. Most university leaders have only the
vaguest idea how many NTT instructors they employ. As one university

analyst put it, "I'm sure [the president] doesn't know how many non-tenure-track faculty are at [university], and he doesn't really care." A provost in another university said, "I don't pay much attention to the number of lecturers, but someone in my office signs off on all lecturer hires." University leaders generally leave these decisions to departments and programs. The decisions to hire lecturers and adjuncts fit what Cohen and March describe as decisions rooted in organizational routines: "The 'decisions' of the system as a whole are a consequence produced by the system but intended by no one and decisively controlled by no one."[2] Real decisions come about, but they grow from invisible roots.

Not every type of academic decision is decentralized, even at large and complex universities. Some decisions are directly controlled by boards, presidents, or provosts, but hiring NTT faculty is rarely one of them. When we review the factors that drive departments at research universities to hire NTT faculty, we necessarily confront the question of who is minding the store: is anyone monitoring, let alone controlling, the overall use of NTT faculty on campus and their conditions of employment?

In this chapter, we describe the factors that lead to decisions to hire NTT faculty to teach undergraduate students in our most prestigious universities. To place the processes used to make these hiring decisions in context, we turn first to a general description of decision making in university settings when the university is a leading research institution. What we have understood for a long time belies the simple but widely held view that university executives direct the hiring of NTT faculty to save money in a resource-constrained environment.

Centralized and Decentralized Decision Making on Campus

The use of NTT faculty for university instruction is an academic matter with significance for the fundamental undergraduate educational mission of a university. A number of studies show that university boards and presidents of most research universities are rarely engaged seriously with academic policy at their institutions.[3]

The level of engagement with academic policy does not appear to be a function of formal governance structure. Governance systems varied widely among the institutions in our study. We have state-supported campuses that are members of large (University of California–Berkeley) and small (University of Illinois, University of Michigan, University of Washington) multicampus systems, and a state-supported campus that stands alone (University of Virginia). We have one mixed public/private Ivy (Cornell University) and four private universities (Duke University, Massachusetts Institute of Technology, Northwestern University, and Washington University). In terms of effective executive authority, some schools place most responsibility in the hands of their deans; others place most authority with a single provost. Until recently, one campus had no provost at all, leaving academic matters largely in the hands of deans.

Final authority rests in governing boards, but boards also vary widely and can be self-replicating, appointed, or elected. Some boards focus on fundraising and investments, others are composed of members who hold their positions for political reasons, and some display relatively little knowledge of or interest in the missions of their universities as educational institutions. No single structure appears to be noticeably more effective than any of the others in terms of encouraging academic leaders to become engaged with academic policy. To the extent that differences in engagement exist, they appear to be rooted in the values and interests of specific leaders rather than in the structures of their organizations.[4]

When governing boards become concerned with academic matters, they might be expected to focus on academic policy rather than particular decisions. However, they are much more likely to intrude in a specific decision in athletics, admissions, architectural design, or even parking. Boards commonly vote—if only by consent—on individual faculty promotion and tenure decisions. Occasionally, members express public displeasure with individual course content or faculty views and even criticize departmental hiring decisions. These incidents become the subject of stories in local newspapers and in the *Chronicle of Higher Education* precisely because they conflict openly with traditional academic norms. This type of intrusion can compromise a university's claim to elite status, and we see few such intrusions by boards of our nation's elite universities. Universities with governing boards that intrude on academic matters rarely reach the top tier.

Governing boards tend to be busy with other matters. They have fiduciary responsibility for their institutions; they search for, hire, evaluate, and compensate presidents; private boards and some public boards are deeply involved in fundraising and investments; they set, or at least approve, tuition; they worry about lawsuits and scandals on campus. They spend relatively little time on matters of academic policy. We are unaware of any instance in which a governing board of an elite university seriously considered the size, growth, or conditions of employment of NTT faculty on campus. Indeed, we doubt that board members have any idea how many NTT faculty are employed by their institution and under what conditions—at least until a union organizing drive or lawsuit catches their attention.

Most university presidents also devote little time to academic issues. A 2006 survey of college presidents found that very few select academic issues as one of the top three uses of their time, although many say they would enjoy spending time on academic matters, and some do become involved with selected issues.[5] Instead, the issues that hold most of the attention of presidents are the crises of the moment: scandals (for example, athletic and research), racial incidents, campus protests, student crises (from fights to suicides), alcohol and drug abuse, and lawsuits. Also high on the list are ongoing projects—fundraising, budget building, relations with members of the governing board, construction, and community relations. Public university presidents must add state relations. All of these issues together preempt the attention of most university leaders, leaving decisions about who teaches undergraduates far down their list of priorities.

University leaders have an amazing array of hot-button issues on their agendas at any one time. During our study, four campuses dealt with athletic scandals, one addressed a highly publicized research scandal, another dealt with a Medicare reimbursement scandal, one campus faced severe public criticism for executive pay and perquisites, two had breakdowns in relations between president and board, one fought for affirmative action policies all the way up to the U.S. Supreme Court, all dealt with fallout from negative promotion decisions including one hunger strike, all dealt with issues of racism and challenges to academic freedom, three experienced union actions by graduate student instructors and lecturers, most had student protests (on issues such as human rights, staff working conditions, and the employment practices of manufacturers of athletic footwear), and all had campus tragedies (student suicides, fatal fires, sexual assaults, and others).[6] These issues make front-page headlines, and they demand an enormous amount of time from boards, presidents, provosts, general counsels, and their staffs.

In addition, all of the campuses in our study faced budget challenges and were in various stages of major fundraising campaigns. Seven of ten managed large healthcare enterprises. All public universities managed state relations, which introduced issues of public funding and legislative interference with college policies and practices. All of the universities in our study were involved in federal relations surrounding financial aid policies, earmarked appropriations, international students and faculty, regulatory requirements, tax and federal audit challenges, endowment rules, military recruitment and Reserve Officers' Training Corps (ROTC), the security of student data systems, and grant funding from the National Science Foundation (NSF), the National Institutes of Health (NIH), the Department of Defense (DOD), or other federal agencies. All of the universities in our study had to address "town-gown" issues—some bordering on outright hostility—and all pursued some aspect of internationalization that required high-level relationships with international dignitaries and institutions.

Time and attention are precious resources on campus. Presidents are bombarded with pressing political and economic problems, far more than they have time to address. Anyone who has occupied such a leadership position knows that academic policy rarely reaches the top tier of issues receiving executive attention. Cohen and March describe it this way:

> Particularly in the larger schools, presidents do not appear to have much to say about academic policy. Indeed, the term "policy" is probably somewhat misleading if it conveys a notion of systematic collective decision making. The set of activities that are subsumed under the general term "academic policy" are the organization of academic departments, the organization of the educational program, degree requirements and alternatives, courses and course assignments, and patterns of student education. . . . Presidents and their chief academic subordinates concede that much of the structure of academic policy is determined in the individual departments, realistically, often in the individual classroom.[7]

The 2006 report of the Association of Governing Boards (AGB) on the "State of the Presidency in American Higher Education"[8] recognizes the tendency of university presidents to spend most of their time and energy raising money and dealing with crises. One of the AGB taskforce's seven recommendations to university presidents urges them to "resist the tendency of such demands as fundraising, state politics, or intercollegiate athletics to undermine . . . leadership."[9]

The relatively frequent turnover at the top testifies to the political stresses faced by presidents and provosts. As Padilla and Ghosh demonstrate, for the cohorts of presidents at Association of American Universities (AAU) institutions who were appointed in 1950 to 1954 and in 1985 to 1989, the average length of presidential service in private institutions declined from 11.7 to 8.8 years; for presidents of publics, average tenure declined from 7.8 to 5.7 years.[10] Seven of our ten institutions experienced change at the top between 2000 and 2006, in two cases more than once. Moreover, because the institutions in our study are at or near the top of the leadership food chain and therefore less likely to be used as stepping stones to other presidential positions, these numbers likely *understate* the frequency of position hopping among institutions that are a step lower in the reputational hierarchy. Half the leaders of our ten institutions had left other chancellorships or presidencies to move to their current positions.

The administrative difficulties posed by frequent turnover are exacerbated by the high number of top administrators who are hired from outside the institution. That is the case for the presidents of all of our ten institutions,[11] and it was the case for 80 percent of the four-year institutions surveyed in 2005 by the *Chronicle of Higher Education*.[12] Inevitably, newly hired outside presidents and provosts are unfamiliar with the cultures of their new institutions and need to spend a great deal of time meeting people, establishing good relations with governing boards, putting executive teams in place, and learning about the customs and practices of their new academic homes. Attention to these matters is regarded as vital by the 2006 AGB taskforce:

[Presidents should] cultivate a deep understanding of the institution and build on its unique character, history, and values. [They should] deliberately work to understand the institution's "narrative" and build support for its next chapters in ways that engage those traditions and the people who have helped create them.[13]

[Boards should] help the president establish and maintain continuity with the institution's tradition and achievements—to connect with and build upon its "saga." It should encourage the president to acquire a deep understanding of the institution's unique values and to pursue a future that engages that tradition.[14]

A second, less obvious fact is that administrators who are hired from the outside do not initially have the personal sense of loyalty to the institution that is more typical of insiders. Boards that have successfully recruited new presidents from outside rarely recognize that by doing so they have learned something about those individuals—that given the right incentives, they are moveable. Such leaders can equally well be hired away—perhaps just when they have finally acquired effective knowledge of how their institutions work. The most vulnerable institutions in this sense are the public universities, which lose their presidents to private institutions that generally enjoy larger endowments, compensate more generously, and avoid many of the political stresses of dealing with partisan boards and legislatures.[15] The 2006 AGB report urges university boards to "eliminate the conditions that often work against internal candidates for the presidency."[16]

The pool of provosts is a popular one from which to recruit presidents. Since few presidencies are filled from within, an ambitious provost will move on to another institution as soon as possible. This encourages administrative conservatism. Provosts with presidential ambitions are loath to create controversies that will antagonize faculty. They know that presidential search committees will hear from unhappy faculty and that negative feedback can compromise their future candidacies.

With changes in presidents come changes in provosts and deans, especially at public institutions. At our ten institutions, six experienced turnover of provosts between 2000 and 2006, and four of them (all publics) had more than two provosts over that short period. Nearly all of the institutions experienced changes in deans of engineering and of arts and sciences. Some provosts and deans were campus insiders, but, even so, frequent turnover of academic leadership makes long-term policy implementation difficult.

The Association of Governing Boards regards changing an entire leadership team with every change of president as an additional serious impediment to any president's ability to provide effective academic leadership. The 2006 AGB report recommends (1) that presidents should "avoid wholesale housecleaning of the executive leadership team in favor of personal choices who may exhibit loyalty but have little understanding or appreciation of the institutions" and should "create an environment that encourages leadership development within the institutions" and (2) that boards should "charge the president with developing opportunities and pathways for leaders to advance within the institution" and "regularly assess leadership development practices and the quality and potential of future institutional leaders."[17] Despite these urgings, housecleaning is more the rule than the exception when new presidents are named at our nation's prestigious research institutions. In the environments we observed, anyone would have difficulty giving sustained attention to more than one or two long-range policy issues. Even if some aspect of academic policy should make that short list, sustained interest may last only as long as the term of appointment of the president or provost in question.

In contrast, regular (tenured) faculty members *expect* to make the academic decisions in research universities. Even though the ultimate authority may rest with university leadership, faculty members make academic decisions and expect them to stick. Moreover, because the setting of academic policies rarely receives higher-level attention, faculty decisions are often made without consistency or attention to university-wide standards. In essence, policy results from the accumulation of individual decisions and the precedents they set, even if they are contradictory and counterproductive at the level of the college or university as a whole. Decisions to hire non-tenure-track faculty are typical of this process; they usually are left to an associate chair of a department or even to a staff member.

Tenured faculty members at these universities are primarily concerned with their research, their teaching, and their students. They jealously guard their prerogatives when it comes to key academic matters such as curriculum, faculty hiring and promotion, and course content. Experienced administrators understand this. They know that they have little direct control over the day-to-day activities of tenured faculty, and they acknowledge having only limited control over the academic evolution of their institutions. Distinguished faculty members are powers to be reckoned with, and administrators feel vulnerable to forceful and articulate expressions of faculty disapproval. The more distinguished (and mobile) the faculty, the greater the prestige of the institution's president off campus, but that same distinguished faculty constrains what the president can accomplish on campus in the academic sphere without faculty support.

No institution with such an ambiguous distribution of authority and uncertain assignment of responsibility in core mission areas is going to have an easy time governing itself. Presidents who come to higher education from the private sector often lack adequate understanding of academic norms and often find relations with faculty to be problematic. None of our ten distinguished universities seriously considered candidates for the presidency who lacked prior experience in higher education.

The Drivers of Non-Tenure-Track Hiring

Even though presidents and provosts rarely have direct control over academic matters, many of their actions and decisions in other arenas have *indirect* consequences for academic decisions. For example, certain choices about budgets and enrollments indirectly promote non-tenure-track hiring at the department level. This is so even when university presidents explicitly say they want to *reduce* the presence of NTT faculty on their campuses. We observed seven types of choices made at the highest administrative levels that created indirect incentives for departments to hire more non-tenure-track faculty.

1. Asymmetric Errors in Enrollments

Although undergraduate student enrollments have increased at all but one of our ten universities over the past decade,[18] the growth is not always acknowledged to be intentional. Admissions offices point to the imperfect predictability of their models, but the errors and their consequences are asymmetric. The costs of falling short of an enrollment goal are politically and financially much more serious than the costs of exceeding the goal. Moreover, the costs of overshooting and the costs of undershooting fall on different parts of the institution. *Under*producing creates an immediate budgetary shortfall and draws the attention of presidents, provosts, and governing boards to the inadequate performance of the admissions office; *over*producing puts pressure on housing, advising, and class size and availability. The financial cost of educating the extra student is much less than the average cost per student; therefore, extra students generate discretionary dollars. Not surprisingly, then, the admission system tends to commit far more "errors" in the direction of exceeding rather than falling short of admissions targets. Indeed, exceeding an enrollment goal may be celebrated as an indication of institutional desirability and quality rather than as a potential liability.[19] As one of our engineering deans put it, "We always have a target enrollment for the engineering school, and we always exceed it."

The problem with this scenario is that the resulting growth in student numbers is not part of any systematic planning.[20] It is seen as an outgrowth of unanticipated temporary "errors," even though cumulative errors can mean substantial growth in undergraduate enrollments over the years. If the growth were an ingredient of a plan, we might expect some pressure to accommodate the additional students with more tenure-track faculty. The mythology of "unexpected" or "temporary" enrollment increases means that universities are reluctant to hire additional faculty with expectations of continued employment. The "extra" students mean more tuition revenue, but they also mean larger courses or a need for alternative instructors to offer additional courses. The consequence is a demand for "temporary" NTT instructors who often end up staying so long that they become permanent.

2. Rigid Control of Tenure-Track Faculty Positions

Rigid control over the number of tenure-track faculty positions limits the number of tenured or tenure-track faculty who can be hired. If positions are not available to be filled, extra students have to be accommodated in some other way. Position controls may keep the number of tenured lines relatively constant, or in the face of financial pressures, position controls may be used to freeze hiring or slow it down so that faculty members who leave, retire, or die are not replaced quickly or at all. Generally, non-tenure-track hires do not count against the total number of positions permitted. Someone has to teach the students. If more permanent faculty cannot be hired, then hiring "temporary" NTT faculty or graduate teaching assistants are alternatives.

3.   Skepticism toward Newly Emerging Fields

Both faculty and administrators are inclined to be suspicious of new fields that do not have long-standing places in the traditional curriculum. Fields such as film, video, animation, and comparative media may be regarded as fads rooted in a superficial popular culture rather than as new disciplines. One can easily forget that many of today's classics had similar beginnings in popular entertainment. The belief that some fields are temporarily popular leads universities to provide them with temporary staff, which means non-tenure-track faculty.

Even if a new field is seen as legitimate and long-lasting, the pool of potential tenure-track faculty may initially be thin. That too encourages hiring temporary non-tenure-track faculty to teach for a number of years while the field matures. In some fields (such as creative writing, film, and theater), active practitioners may be thought to be the most effective teachers. Since successful practitioners rarely want to devote all of their time to teaching, they are more easily attracted by offers of part-time, NTT employment.

4.   Limitations on Numbers of Teaching Assistants

The shortage of tenure-track faculty positions nationally has led to concerns about placement opportunities for PhDs, and some provosts and deans press departments to limit the sizes of their graduate populations. The total numbers of graduate students at all of our institutions have increased, but the growth is heavily skewed toward the science and engineering fields, where growing research dollars provide more money for research assistants and where many PhDs seek employment in industry rather than academe. Shrinkage in graduate student numbers is most prevalent in humanities and social science fields, where students are more challenged to find academic jobs after degree completion.

Further downward pressure on the size of certain graduate populations comes from increasing competition for the best graduate students. Competition creates pressure to provide more generous funding packages, and this in turn reduces the numbers of students who can be supported. Most humanities and social science programs at the nation's elite research universities are now offering five- or six-year funding packages. This in turn has led to smaller entering cohorts of graduate students and fewer students available to serve as teaching assistants. These are also the departments with talented students who win a disproportionate number of outside graduate fellowships from the National Science Foundation, from privately endowed funds, or from elsewhere. Success with outside funding allows departments to take more students, but the fellowships mean that students are unavailable to serve as teaching assistants.

In science and engineering fields, the dynamics are different but still result in fewer available graduate teaching assistants. The numbers of graduate students have risen, but the increase is supported by funding for research and training. Federal training grants often specify that students on the grants must not serve as teaching assistants. Growing research funds deflect graduate students from teaching to research, and increases in graduate student populations in science disciplines increasingly tend to pull tenured faculty away from undergraduate teaching in favor of graduate teaching and mentoring. In some cases, faculty members who supervise large numbers of PhD dissertations will insist that dissertation supervision be counted as a replacement for an undergraduate course.

In sum, whether it is due to intentional reductions in graduate student populations in the humanities or "diversions" of graduate students into research (and away from teaching) in the sciences, there has been a decrease in the available number of teaching assistants for introductory courses at many of the nation's leading universities. To offer undergraduate instruction with a constant number of tenure-track faculty, the number of NTT faculty has grown.

5.   Negotiated Settlements with Graduate Student Unions

Union organizing drives among graduate teaching assistants have been successful at many public institutions.[21] We include this among our list of factors driven by high-level administrators for two reasons. First, the conditions of employment that lead to unionization are primarily the consequence of flawed leadership and inadequate attention to student concerns. Second, the bargained agreements are approved by presidents and provosts who sometimes seek to avoid conflict to such an extent that they make unnecessary concessions. To the extent that these agreements raise the cost of teaching assistants, incentives grow to hire more instructors off the tenure track.

In our view, this incentive has been only modestly influential. Faculty remain fiercely loyal to their graduate students and resist favoring lecturers over teaching assistants in employment unless other sources of graduate funding are available. We discuss union issues in greater detail in chapter 7.

6. Budget "Reforms"

Budget changes have been adopted by some but not all campuses, and they tend to reinforce decentralized decision making. Responsibility-centered management (RCM) swept through higher education in the 1990s.[22] RCM encouraged the placement of responsibility for revenue generation and expenditures with individual colleges within a university (or even with individual departments), and those campuses that embraced its principles established systems that encourage cost-conscious decision making at the college and departmental levels. They also created powerful incentives to engage in practices that were not consciously promoted by the upper administrative levels—the employment of less expensive non-tenure-track faculty; the employment of part-time faculty at small fractions so that they do not qualify for health insurance and other fringe benefits; the offering of high-enrollment courses in subjects regarded as tangential to the central mission of the college (such as English composition courses offered at an engineering school). We address this factor in detail in chapter 6.

7. Competition for Faculty Research Stars

Competition for the best faculty (where *best* is defined in terms of scholarship) entails offering desirable conditions of employment, including attractive salaries, benefits, and employment for partners. High on this list are the number and type of courses required to be taught each year by tenure-track faculty members. Universities compete with each other by reducing this number and permitting mobile faculty to teach in their research specialty, thereby allowing them to devote more and more time to their research.

Teaching loads have fallen significantly for tenure-track faculty in most research universities, and tenured faculty do less undergraduate teaching at the introductory level than they did in the past. This is especially evident in introductory languages, introductory composition, and calculus, but it occurs in all fields. As part of recruitment packages, most elite universities now offer new assistant professors a first year with only two courses and a semester (or even two) of "nurturing leave" free of teaching duties during the pretenure years. In economics, political science, and psychology, normal annual teaching loads at elite research universities have fallen over the past decade from four to three courses per year. Forty years ago, teaching loads in these same fields were often three courses each semester—roughly double what they are today. To retain outstanding faculty in the face of offers from other universities, provosts and deans negotiate over nearly anything, including an individual's teaching responsibilities. Fewer undergraduate courses from tenure-track faculty creates teaching demands that must be met by others while staying within balanced departmental budgets—creating a gap that is often filled by non-tenure-track faculty.

Quite apart from the number of courses *reported* for each TT faculty member per year, some departments have become creative in requiring fewer courses than they report. One department we visited employed a fiction of listing more than twenty "administrative" courses each year to show more TT involvement in formal teaching than was actually occurring; another used a vehicle of "seminars" that met but required no course preparation on the part of the credited faculty member; a third credited courses to TT faculty members when the courses were actually taught by postdoctoral fellows; a number of departments permitted faculty to offer courses regularly despite tiny enrollments. If deans and provosts do not monitor these practices continually and carefully, the number of student credit hours taught by regular tenured faculty can shrink considerably over time. If the TT faculty does not grow in number to compensate for lower course loads, fewer students taught, or a shift in teaching responsibility toward specialized upper-level courses and graduate training, NTT faculty will be hired to make up the shortfall. The significant impact of heightened competition among elite research universities for faculty is discussed in detail in chapter 4.

Monitoring Faculty Trends: Who Is Minding the Store?

The American Association of University Professors (AAUP) took notice of increasing numbers of non-tenure-track faculty as early as 1978.[23] Articles voicing concern about the move toward NTT faculty appeared at various points over the years in *Academe*, the AAUP's journal,[24] along with additional reports in 1986 and 1993.[25]

By the late 1990s, there was sufficient concern about the growth in NTT faculty to capture the attention of the Association of American Universities (AAU), an organization of sixty research universities to which all of the top universities belong. In 1999 and again in 2000, the AAU tenure committee conducted studies of growth in NTT faculty at a sample of AAU institutions.[26] AAU efforts prompted a few of these institutions to begin collecting more systematic information about hiring trends; others merely conducted one-time special data collections to respond to the AAU request. (At least one of the institutions in our study reported data widely regarded as unreliable.) Nonetheless, few elite research universities have taken the sort of action that might have been expected had they regarded the growth in NTT numbers to be a significant problem.

The picture we see is one of highly decentralized decision making that is influenced by policy changes at the top. The policy makers, however, are typically unaware of the full set of consequences of these policy shifts and especially the consequences for the makeup of the instructional workforce.

Four sets of circumstances encourage more systematic monitoring of NTT numbers. The first occurs when NTT faculty members become active in trying to organize their workforce on campus. Somewhat belatedly, university leaders scramble to understand the size, distribution, and working conditions of their NTT faculty. If the organizing push is successful, then the union agreements that result call for careful monitoring. NTT faculty are currently represented by unions at two of our ten institutions, and both of them were organized in the last decade.[27] Non-tenure-track faculty are ripe for organizing and represent one of the arenas of greatest promise and activity for national unions.

A second circumstance that encourages attention to the NTT workforce on a campus arises when a personnel action against a NTT faculty member results in a messy grievance or lawsuit. Only then do some academic administrators who thought they could easily terminate a NTT faculty member learn the limits imposed by faculty culture or state law.

Neither of these first two sets of circumstances suggests a proactive, thoughtful approach. In both cases, university leaders are reacting to situations that they would have preferred to avoid in the first place. A third type of circumstance illustrates what leaders can do in advance of personnel problems to understand the academic workforce. A new president, provost, or dean who arrives on campus from elsewhere sometimes triggers a close look at the numbers and conditions of employment of NTT faculty. For example, one of our universities recruited a president from another institution that employs very few NTT faculty. He was disturbed by what he saw on his new campus and asked for systematic data on NTT faculty employed there. That was the beginning of efforts to collect systematic faculty information in arts and sciences. In two other cases, university leaders were insiders but came from units that employed no NTT faculty. They were similarly surprised and concerned about the numbers of NTT faculty in arts and sciences as a whole and began to collect data.

Finally, when a president and governing board succeed in raising substantial money to make a dramatic move upward in national rankings, they often decide the route is through expanding the TT faculty, sometimes by replacing NTT instructors. The University of Southern California (USC) and New York University (NYU) made such moves in the 1990s. Part of USC's overall strategy was to move core general education requirements into the College of Arts and Sciences and to hire more tenure-track faculty to teach those courses.[28] NYU pursued a similar strategy, first building faculty research strength in the liberal arts during the 1990s and then in 2004 announcing The Partners Fund to raise $210 million in private funds over five years. The fund would pay for hiring 250 faculty members in arts and sciences, 125 of whom would be replacements and 125 of whom would be additions to its 625 faculty in an effort to recenter the university around the liberal arts college.[29]

This strategy is not limited to private universities. In 2006, President Bernard Machen of the University of Florida proposed an Academic Enhancement Program that would add 200 faculty members over time, financing the expansion with an additional $1,000 per year in tuition charges. The proposal's rationale stated that "Improvement in only one parameter—faculty resources (number of faculty, faculty/student ratio, class size)—would very likely move [the University of Florida] into the top 10 public list."[30] In 2008, the governor of New York State proposed adding 2,000 faculty members to the campuses of the State University of New York (SUNY) system and establishing an endowment for the system "to put New York's public universities on a par with those in states like California and Michigan." The estimated cost over thirteen years was $1.6 billion in one-time costs plus $226 million per year.[31]

Presidents of universities below the top twenty know that they cannot hope to join the ranks of elite institutions without gaining control of their NTT numbers. This strategic focus on shifting from NTT to TT as a way of increasing prestige has less relevance for our ten premier universities, which are already highly ranked and which compete on factors other than the number of NTT faculty employed.

In most cases, the short answer to our question about who is minding the store is "No one." A lack of attention to the overall character of an institution's teaching faculty can have seriously negative consequences for universities. We turn to a discussion of implications and consequences in chapter 8. But first we elaborate on four critical factors in higher education today that are driving changes in the makeup of the instructional workforce—the nature of competition and the market (chapters 4 and 5), the use of business thinking and the unanticipated consequences of popular budgetary reforms (chapter 6), and unionization in the academy (chapter 7).

4

From Monastery to Market

In spite of resistance from many quarters, the term *competition* is arising more and more frequently in the discourse of higher education. Not only has there been an enormous expansion in the demand for higher education over the last fifty years, but awareness has grown that in a large and fluid market, every participant will face a heightened competition for place and resources. Students compete for places in their preferred colleges, colleges compete for the most attractive student applicants and the most prestigious faculty, and faculty compete for attractive posts. All of these participants are aware that the market has become much larger and tougher and that new players with different skills and needs may threaten the security of their own places in the system.

In addition to the word *competition*, other terminology has been drawn from commerce to describe every aspect of college and university life. Students become consumers. Universities compete for them in an applicant market and then place them after graduation in a job market. Higher-education performance is to be assessed in terms of concrete outcome measures that can be used to evaluate whether state legislatures should continue to provide support.[1] Colleges and universities are urged to develop business models, to create financing systems that mirror those used in business and to devote energy and resources to developing an effective brand. These linguistic changes appall many who remember and value the abstract intellectual roots of higher education and who decry how far we have traveled along the road from the monastery to the market.[2]

The changes are real and not simply linguistic. University admissions offices are acutely aware of market competition. They routinely compile lists of the universities to which they lose applicants and against which their recruitment efforts are most often successful. Development offices, especially in private universities, employ hundreds of fundraisers, many of whom do not have backgrounds in education. Administrators at all levels (especially, but not exclusively, in finance areas) are increasingly drawn from business and finance rather than higher education.[3] In this chapter, we consider the effects of market competition on university hiring practices. In chapter 6, we turn to actions taken by university leadership to import business thinking and models into university life.

No one should be surprised that for-profit institutions have entered an educational arena that is evolving toward a business model. Moreover, this move enjoys the political support of many federal and state officials.[4] The most prestigious of our traditional colleges and universities take comfort in the belief that they are not likely to lose significant numbers of their regular undergraduate or graduate students to for-profit colleges. Yet even some of these universities enhance their financial strength with evening programs, continuing education programs, and summer programs, all of which are vulnerable to competition from lower-cost and more convenient profit-making institutions. The University of Illinois, for example, is developing an online campus called the Global Campus that will eventually enroll more students than on-site enrollment at the system's three campuses combined. University officials estimated that 60 to 70 percent of instructors would be "nontraditional faculty."[5]

This much broader market and the revised functions and expectations of higher education have led to an increased reliance on non-tenure-track faculty. The large numbers of NTT faculty nationally represent a fundamental change in the structure of higher education that cannot be reversed easily through the efforts of administrators or legislators who support public universities. The belief that university leaders should simply decide to hire only faculty who are on the tenure track is wholly inconsistent with the forces that are driving these changes. We address below the historical changes in the market context of higher education that have fueled the hiring of non-tenure-track faculty.

Changing Student Demographics

Over the last fifty years, undergraduate enrollments increased dramatically in the United States, and the *number* of institutions of higher education increased as well. How did our economy, wealthy as it is, manage to pay for this growth? Higher education is inherently expensive. The cost of instruction and fees must be covered, and time spent in study is time not spent in the labor force. In the early years of private colleges and universities in the United States, the few students who attended came from families that were able to pay the costs. The public universities that served less well-heeled students were smaller than they are now, and they were able to maintain low tuition rates through the generous support of state legislatures that placed high social value on education.

Growth in higher-education enrollments occurred after World War II, financed largely through the GI Bill and through the savings that students and their families had accumulated during the war years. The expansion continued to be fueled by the tremendous increase in national prosperity that took place after the war.

This fuel is clearly running out. Tuition costs have been rising much more rapidly than inflation, and state legislatures are displaying less and less willingness to increase their support in proportion to cost. Every public university in our study can demonstrate that public funds cover a declining share of its costs, and each one is increasing tuition and private fundraising efforts to make up the difference. The increase in tuition has in turn increased the burdens on students and their families. Over the years, there has been a gradual increase in reliance on borrowing, and many of today's graduates leave college with substantial debt.[6]

This change in circumstance reflects a change in attitude toward the mission of higher education. During the 1960s and 1970s, economists who were interested in labor-market behavior began generating sophisticated studies of the "returns" to higher education.[7] Because the most easily measured returns are those with an economic base, the studies concentrated on the income-earning potential that they believed to be conferred by a college degree. This kind of comparison has become commonplace, and the higher-education literature is filled with demonstrations that a bachelor's degree will make possible a career-long income that will more than cover its cost.[8] These demonstrations in turn are used to justify the heavy loan burdens that many students today accept. From this perspective, borrowing to support an education is analogous to borrowing to buy a house.

More recently, some state governments have demanded that public higher education demonstrate significant contributions to the economic vitality of the state and region. Both public and private universities have responded to these pressures. As evidence of their contributions, they cite a skilled workforce that remains in the area, start-up companies, technology transfers, private investment, and federal dollars flowing to states as a consequence of university initiatives.[9]

The published demonstrations of high returns to education are not flawless, and a good statistical case can be made that they are overly optimistic, but that does not concern us here. A by-product of these studies is that they have tended to narrow the perceived mission of higher education itself. Historically, liberal arts education was defended partly because it was seen as a contributor to quality of life, partly because it enhanced career flexibility, and partly because it promised to provide an educated public—a prerequisite for a successfully functioning democracy. If the goal of higher education now is to enhance career income and if that enhanced income justifies taking on debt, then students and their parents will seek proof that the education offered by a university meets this much more narrow economic purpose. They can be expected to compare schools on criteria different from those of the past and to apply a more consciously economic calculus to their enrollment choices.

This tendency is enhanced by the demographic changes that have accompanied enrollment growth. Two generations ago, a college education was closely associated with students who came from upper socioeconomic backgrounds. Indeed, social status and college education were so closely linked that preparation for a social role was often deliberately integrated into student activities. Increased access to higher education necessarily has introduced new socioeconomic groups into colleges, and the educational goals of these new students are not the same as the goals of those who entered college two generations ago. Hand in hand with

this growth is an undergraduate population that is far more heteroge-
neous than it was fifty years ago.[10] The almost universal demise of the
"core curriculum" constitutes an institutional acknowledgment of how
difficult it is to devise a curriculum that is equally suitable for all members
of such a diverse population of students.

hmm

It is dangerous to paint with too broad a brush, but a generalization
that frequently appears in informal academic conversations is that the
students who entered the elite colleges and universities of the past were
not driven primarily by a concern for jobs. They came from professional
backgrounds with educated and relatively successful parents who
expected their children to become well-educated as undergraduates and,
at least for their sons, to prepare for professional careers in law or
medical school afterward. The development of the liberal arts as a foundation for a college curriculum was nurtured by this environment.

Student participants in higher education today have different backgrounds. Some of them see the liberal arts not as personally and intellectually broadening opportunities but as barriers that interfere with the
acquisition of skills that are required for future employment. This per-
ception can turn into resentment when it is compounded by an awareness
of the debt burden that will be imposed by college and of the number
of required classes that do not generate obvious financial returns.

A focus on the economic returns of higher education to the state and
region has encouraged more and more emphasis in universities on science,
engineering, business, and the health professions. Every major university
seems to have a life science initiative—not only because of the intellectual
vitality of the field and funding from the National Institutes of Health
but also because it is seen as a vehicle to invigorate local and state
economies with high-tech biology-based companies. Governors, state
legislators, university presidents, and governing board members hope
that the life sciences will produce in their area the Silicon Valley or
Massachusetts Miracle of the twenty-first century.

eg

These changing circumstances have not been greeted with enthusiasm
by all tenure-track faculty. Established faculty in arts and sciences are
strongly inclined to preserve the idealism embedded in the traditional
elite liberal arts university model. They continue to argue vehemently
for the preservation of traditional course requirements (in literature,

languages, mathematics, history, and so on), regardless of the interests and goals of students. As a result, adaptation to change is taking place through adaptation in the teaching force itself—that is, through the use of NTT faculty, many of whom are not strongly committed to traditional liberal arts values. As consumers influence what is produced and how it is produced in every market, so to some degree do students shape certain curriculum changes when they choose institutions that promise to serve their perceived needs. Through this market mechanism, students (and their parents) influence what is to be taught and how it is taught.[11] In short, changing demographics have created a market in flux, and markets in flux typically create new institutions. In this case, the rapid expansion in the presence of for-profit colleges and the use of non-tenure-track faculty are prominent examples.

Broadening Markets from Local to National to International

A second major change in higher education is the extent of the market for higher-education services. Modern technology has transformed local academic markets into national and international markets. This is especially true for students who attend college as residential students rather than commuters from home. A prospective student can use the Internet to "visit" any number of alternative colleges, getting a flavor of their curricular styles, learning about the communities in which they are located, and downloading extensive details about size, diversity, sports, social activities, living costs, and so on. Transportation costs are no longer the barriers to choice that they once were, and a prospective student can reasonably compare the apparent merits of one college 50 miles away to those of another 2,000 miles away. In short, the market for students has become far more open.[12]

The market for faculty is now international. Compared with many other employee groups, college and university faculty have always been mobile, with faculty moving from one college or university to another. However, before the modern era, such moves were cumbersome. The transportation of an entire household was expensive and awkward, communications were not as fluid as they are now, and the traditions of long-term job stability and loyalty to an institution were strong. The massive academic and professional association meetings that now play an active role in position search and relocation did not exist. Our modern system of faculty who split appointments between two universities located on different coasts (or even continents) did not exist, and large numbers of new PhDs did not traverse the nation giving job talks. Now, modern comprehensive communication systems allow faculty to review alternative opportunities and employment conditions in a matter of hours. Given the concomitant reduction in the cost and inconvenience associated with physical mobility, faculty members no longer regard their university positions as lifetime commitments.

Did they ever?

These two changes in market circumstance have pushed top-tier colleges and universities into an intensely competitive environment. Indeed, observing this competition has become a national pastime. The obvious example is sports, but even competition for faculty is occasionally newsworthy. Over the last decade, leading newspapers have published front-page stories of prominent faculty recruited (or almost recruited) from university to university. In some cases, the stories are accompanied by speculations of astonishingly high salaries.[13] Today, universities compete on nearly everything, including the size of their fundraising campaigns, the size of annual returns on endowment, the number of National Merit Scholars in their student body, the average student scores on SATs, the luxury of residence halls, and the provision of iPods.

Given our national fascination for lists and rankings, it is not surprising that this competition is reported in the media as ranking—both in sports and in institutional quality. Admissions officers are convinced that the national visibility attributable to successful sports programs substantially increases student applications. Perhaps even more critical to the competitive well-being of academic institutions is the ranking of four-year institutions that is published by student advisory manuals, most prominently by *U.S. News & World Report*. The effect of these publications on students' selections of undergraduate colleges is substantial.[14] Colleges and universities themselves place enormous importance on their own academic rankings, whether they are released by the National Research Council or by national disciplinary societies. In one of our interviews, after we exchanged introductions with a prominent department chair, his first comment was "We're number one!" The entire hour of that interview centered on national ranking and the research that supported it. The word *teaching* did not arise at all. This was an extreme case, but it was not unusual in substance. A university president greeted us with a humbler statement: "We were just ranked in the top three. Now we need to improve ourselves so we deserve to be there!"

One need only observe the substantial institutional resources devoted to preparing for the periodic National Research Council ranking exercise to understand how important such rankings are. They are never far from the consciousness of graduate students, faculty, or administrators. Institutional stature is no longer only a matter of local pride or casual interest. It influences the allocation of personnel and resources, and, given the willingness and ability of both faculty and students to move from one school to another, it is rapidly becoming a matter of institutional survival.

Rank and Hierarchy

Economists have long believed that competition among American businesses—especially those oriented toward retail consumer products—has led to exaggerations in product differences that are designed to attract and retain consumer loyalty. In this view, products ranging from automobiles, computers, and kitchen appliances to razors and toothpaste are much more similar in quality and performance than their producers would have us believe. Moreover, this drive to differentiate one's product is not merely happenstance; it is a natural consequence of the competitive environment. Competitors are driven to differentiate their products as means for attracting and retaining customers.

We see the same behavior in the aggressively competitive environment of higher education. The product in this case is education itself coupled with the more or less unique life experiences that are common to residential undergraduate settings. The implication is that institutions will seek to create unique identities that will lead students and faculty to believe that the differences are much greater than in fact is justified. That one library boasts 4 million volumes and another only half as many cannot possibly have any influence over the quality of education received by the typical undergraduate; nevertheless, library collection size shows up in almost all recruiting brochures.

This means that resources come to be committed to image enhancement as well as to product improvement. This, in turn, means that expenditures that tend to attract students and faculty away from other institutions are seen to be as useful as expenditures that would tend to improve education or increase access by serving more students and faculty. It is not by chance that the word *brand* has become commonplace in university admissions offices.

The competition for students goes beyond simple recruitment. Subsidies are given to nationally visible sports teams; large sums are spent on upscale dormitories, cafeterias, and recreational centers; and public relations departments are allotted large budgets. The economic cost of what has come to be called the "amenities arms race" has not been measured, but we cannot be surprised that tuition costs are rising as fast as they are or that even apparently well-funded educational institutions appear to be under continual financial stress. In our view, this is the natural result of a significant increase in competitiveness in the market for students. In this sense, the rapid rise in tuition charges in recent years is not entirely attributable to increases in the costs of energy, health care, or technical resources. It is also attributable to the cost of product differentiation—upscale dormitories (which are themselves reflections of student demand), modern recreational facilities, prominent sports teams, and the public relations efforts that are necessary to convince students and parents that these differences are important and unique.

This leads to the second element of the economist's insight—that is, this competitive process tends to place institutions in difficult economic circumstances. They are driven to use any available resources to enhance their competitive positions. Mailings, brochures, Web sites, staff visits, and college days are all committed to the competitive recruitment of students. A recent study by Noel-Levitz concluded that the average four-year private college spends over $2,000 in recruitment costs for every newly enrolled student.[15] Public institutions spend perhaps a quarter as much, but even this is far higher than the $75 that is typical of two-year colleges, which are insulated by status and geography from such intense competition.

"Difficult economic circumstances" inevitably extend to instructional staff, including tenure-track faculty. It is hard to quantify and compare the workloads and stress levels of faculty today with those faced by faculty several decades ago, but today tenured and tenure-track faculty at elite universities are subject to tremendous pressures. Research activities extend into evenings and weekends, committee assignments are often burdensome, and the pressures to perform in the classroom have become acute. Workload and job stress are now topics of everyday conversation throughout academia. This is another aspect of the increasingly competitive environment. Tenure-track faculty members share in the institutional stress that these more active markets have engendered.

Competition in higher education rests on *hierarchy*—the strongest research program, the best sports program, the most active social life, the best teachers, the most up-to-date technology, and so on. Rankings are usually compressed into one summary statistic that is distributed in a national news magazine, by the National Research Council, or by disciplinary societies. As a foundation for competition, however, hierarchy is much more demanding than business success in commercial markets. A high place in a hierarchy is by its nature scarce. Barring occasional ties, only ten institutions can be placed in the top ten. We encountered few administrators in our interviews who did not feel that membership in the top ten was a reasonable aspiration for the overall university and for each individual field on their campuses. This aspiration was never accompanied by a mention of which other institution might have its own rank lowered as a consequence of one's own rise, nor was it explained why these other institutions would not take equally aggressive steps to preserve their positions.

This aspect of competition places research universities under great stress. They are the ones that are most often ranked. Once the focus has shifted away from ordinary market success or product quality to rank, competitive pressures cease to encourage efficiency and instead foster combat. Compared to business competition, in which growth is possible when markets grow, positions in a hierarchy are necessarily zero-sum. The dean who devotes extraordinary resources to recruiting nationally known philosophers and announces proudly that the effort has raised the local philosophy department to number one in the country is rarely concerned that the same great expenditure and effort has reduced the ranking of the philosophy department at some other university to number two (and perhaps the former number two to three, number three to four, and so on). From a national standpoint, what has been accomplished? What may have been an enormous resource commitment will serve no additional students. It has built no new buildings, and it will not likely change the quantity or quality of research carried out in philosophy as a discipline. What it will do is enhance the reputation of one university compared to another, raise a few salaries, and cost a lot of money.

This is exactly what the classic economic model would lead us to expect. Expenses are incurred that differentiate the university's own product, that provide little of national value, and that leave the university financially stressed. They also drive up selected faculty salaries in a spiral of competition—while faculty members compete fiercely among themselves to become the ones who benefit. Salary plus benefits above $250,000 for a distinguished senior faculty member are no longer unusual at leading research universities. A full professor might also occupy an endowed chair with $25,000 to $100,000 per year of discretionary funding for research. Beginning assistant professors in economics now start at $130,000 plus benefits; in engineering, over $100,000 plus benefits. The costs of space can be even greater, although these are one-time dollars and not annually recurring expenses. The average start-up costs for a new hire in the laboratory sciences at one of our schools was nearly $700,000, plus lab renovation of nearly $200,000. For a distinguished senior hire, the costs can be even greater, including dedicated support for graduate students.

The competition for outstanding faculty unquestionably enhances their incomes. This observation naturally leads to another. If these widely publicized salaries are high relative to other professions, does this not attract more students into faculty careers? The answer is not entirely clear. The particular salaries in this case are generated not by a desire for *more* faculty (the traditional economic explanation for a price increase) but by a desire to recruit the *best* faculty. Those who are not deemed to be the best and who are not the targets of aggressive competitive recruiting are left either with the salaries that might have been in place without the competition or, because of budget constraints, with a worse situation than they would have had otherwise.[16] In less well-endowed private universities and especially in public universities that have lower endowments and declining financial support from the state, competition for stars consumes financial resources, leaving less for other faculty. This is part of the financial imperative that drives hiring choices toward less expensive NTT faculty.

One final and discouraging insight that can be drawn from this description is that the university can do little about it. The competitive behavior just described is not easily avoided. Many see it as a matter of survival as a top-tier institution. Failure to compete would entail the loss of outstanding faculty and outstanding student prospects along with them. The situation is a heightened version of what is familiar in markets for consumer products. Consumer-product corporations advertise because they know that if they do not, they will ultimately fail. For the same reason, American institutions of higher education that do not continue to strive to maintain their status relative to their peers will quickly move down into the second tier.

The Academic Labor Market: Risk, Rent, and Compensation

For generations, one of the first propositions presented to beginning students of economics is that there is no essential market link between market price and value. Once they hear about Alfred Marshall's diamond-water paradox (that diamonds are of relatively little real importance but carry high prices, while water is essential to life and is virtually free), students recognize that scarcity is the critical determinant of market price, and the paradox comes to be seen as no paradox at all.

That insight frequently evaporates when the context shifts from the abstract examples of economics classes to real situations. There is a strong social tendency to associate price with value—to assume that the more expensive automobile must be a "better" automobile. When this inference is extended to individual compensation, salary differences become value differences and ultimately status differences. Applied to the academic context, this can turn into a serious misunderstanding. As individuals, untenured lecturers and adjuncts are often highly valued by their employers at research institutions. Some untenured lecturers are honored and respected more highly than better-compensated tenured colleagues, especially those who are no longer at the top of their scholarly specialties. In this sense, lecturers are not always second-class citizens. They are intellectually active, they are effective teachers, they inspire their students, and they embody the goals of their institutions just as do tenured faculty.

Many non-tenure-track faculty at elite research universities also engage in research and write books and articles. Those in the studio arts produce and sell works of art. Those in performance areas participate in stage productions. They encourage and support their students in their own research and individual intellectual development. Where they fail is in achieving a ranking in the research hierarchy that is high enough to contribute significantly to the visibility of their institutions.[17] This is especially true at leading research universities. A non-tenure-track lecturer who claims to perform the same duties as a tenured faculty member is often challenged (at least rhetorically) to undergo a tenure review similar to that experienced by tenured colleagues. Tenured and untenured faculty members alike recognize that such a review would almost certainly fail because the research, even if it is plentiful, would not achieve the standards expected by the tenure system.

To succeed in a tenure review, a teaching specialist would need a review process different from the one used for teacher-scholars. Different criteria would have to be established (for example, contributions to research on pedagogy published in journals or books that focus on such material), and different types of internal and external reviewers would have to be selected. A few of the elite universities have attempted to establish different procedures, and some have awarded tenure to such specialists on a limited basis, but most have not done so.[18]

We see no signs that competition among elite universities for rankings will abate. The enormous endowments of some private and a few public institutions provide the resources to a select few for "upping the ante."[19] Investments in building world-class universities in Asia and Europe will add to the mix. University leaders will be challenged to decide when, where, and under what conditions to compete. Not every highly ranked institution competes in medicine or engineering; not every one invests in nationally televised sports programs; not every highly ranked university competes for faculty members (even if they are distinguished) who refuse to engage with undergraduate students; not every one chooses to offer courses in all of the same languages or fields of study. Making decisions not to compete are never easy, especially for leaders of institutions vying for top-ten rankings. We return to this challenge in our concluding chapter. Next, we turn to the market for non-tenure-track faculty.

5

The Market for Non-Tenure-Track Instruction

Hiring NTT Instructors: The Demand Side

Three broad categories of instructor meet the teaching needs of a modern research university—tenure-track (TT) faculty, various designations of non-tenure-track (NTT) (including part-time) instructors, and graduate student teaching assistants (TAs). Understanding the market for non-tenure-track instruction requires considering how these three types of instructors fit together. Are they interchangeable? If they are, then cost changes in one may lead to offsetting employment changes in another. To give a direct example, if non-tenure-track instructors receive a significant boost in salary (perhaps as a consequence of unionization), can we expect a university to shift its employment emphasis toward other suppliers of instruction (graduate students or tenure-track faculty), or will the university absorb the new costs without making accommodating changes in teaching staff?[1]

Our limited sample of ten universities (and the lack of significant recent changes in relative cost among the three instructional types) will not support a statistical study of substitutability across the three categories. However, our detailed interviews did shed light on how administrators think about and choose among instructional types. We begin with three general observations.

First, our inquiries about the possibility of substitution did not uncover particularly high levels of sophistication. Few administrators had enough information to compare costs across the three instructional types, particularly because of the differing arrays of benefit and tuition-waiver costs that are attached to the three types of instructor. Without a fairly well-developed awareness of relative costs, it is hard to see how deliberate, price-driven substitutions can take place. That does not mean that substitution is absent, but it is certainly not high on the administrative agenda, and to the extent that it does take place, it is unlikely to be based on well-informed analysis.

Second, the three instructor types fill different academic roles. Non-tenure-track instructors are usually described as "teaching only" staff. Formal job descriptions for the teaching specialists focus on teaching obligations, and although "service" and "intellectual development" (research) may occasionally be mentioned, these elements have little significance in their employment contracts. By contrast, those who hold tenure-track positions in a research university face stringent demands for research productivity, graduate instruction, and service. Their job descriptions are different from those of non-tenure-track instructors and go well beyond teaching alone.

Third, the decisions to hire each of these three instructional types are made at different times by different people according to different rules. Tenure-track hiring is a long and arduous process. Faculty positions require national searches; the negotiations, successful or not, can extend over weeks or months; and if the recruitment is not successful, the negotiation, if not the entire search, begins all over again. In the case of senior hires, the process can take years. The department faculty, the dean of the school or college, various other committees, and sometimes the provost, president, and vice presidents (for example, of research) are involved.

Graduate student recruiting is much more streamlined: targets are set, applications are received, decisions and offers are made, and students decide in a process that takes less than a year. A graduate school may be involved, but most of the action in graduate student recruiting takes place in the department, program, or even subareas of the discipline. Typically, a faculty member or faculty committee is designated within each department to handle graduate admissions, and most of the decisions are made there.

The time frame for recruitment of non-tenure-track teaching faculty is shorter still. This process may be run by an associate chair or a staff member who is responsible for seeing that necessary courses are taught. Rarely are searches national in scope. They can occur much more quickly, may be ad hoc in nature, and may be started and completed during the month or even the week before classes begin.

We encountered occasional conjectures that the sizes of some graduate programs are driven by the need for teaching assistants in undergraduate classes. At the same time, much stronger evidence suggests that the characteristics of a graduate program are determined largely by other factors. Faculty members at research universities see graduate students as critical to their own intellectual and teaching aspirations. The norm—especially in the humanities and the social sciences—is that any faculty member who wishes should have some number (which varies by discipline) of graduate students to work "with" him or her but that "too many" students can impose an undue burden. In the sciences, the number of graduate students is overwhelmingly driven by research dollars. Thus, in most universities, the faculty members at the department level ultimately determine the size of their graduate programs.

In a few cases, we spoke with graduate deans who expressed concern that some graduate programs were too large to maintain quality or to result in proper job placement. More than one dean claimed to have exerted control over program size, but we had difficulty confirming that the claimed control had much impact. The most effective devices used to limit the size of graduate cohorts are financing schemes that encourage departments to improve the competitiveness of their graduate financial aid offers. These schemes lead to higher costs per student—by encouraging increases in the proportion of fellowships as compared with teaching assignments and also increases in the duration of the financial aid commitments. This usually means that departmental resources can support fewer graduate students, but it still leaves the final responsibility for numbers in the hands of the department. If departments can support more students—with training grants, research funds, or endowed or externally funded fellowships—then they admit them, and no graduate dean we interviewed was willing to interfere.

In any case, the concerns expressed by graduate deans had nothing to do with the need for teaching resources but were derived instead from a concern for the quality and career prospects of PhD recipients. Particularly in the humanities and some of the social sciences, where there is evidence of oversupply in the academic market as a whole, deans

encourage downsizing individual programs. Although reducing graduate
student numbers (and consequently the numbers of available teaching
assistants) would likely require using non-tenure-track faculty as replacements, we were given few reasons to believe that this substitution possibility drives decisions about the sizes of graduate student cohorts.

In most of our example institutions (particularly the publicly supported universities), the need for undergraduate instruction has grown
substantially over the last decade. This growth has led almost exclusively
to increases in the numbers of non-tenure-track faculty. Although the
 numbers of tenure-track faculty and the sizes of graduate programs have
remained remarkably stable (especially outside of the sciences), the ranks
of non-tenure-track faculty have grown as the increased teaching
needs of the institutions have grown. Even in the sciences, in which
numbers of graduate students have grown, the growth has been driven
by expanded opportunities for research support, leaving increases in
undergraduate enrollments to be handled by non-tenure-track faculty.

The size of a tenure-track faculty is usually governed by an intricate
set of administrative processes, and these processes are unquestionably
in place because of concerns about cost as well as quality. Regular tenure-
track faculty members represent collectively the greatest cost element
in higher education, and administrators are acutely conscious of this
expense. Concerns about cost lead universities to keep tight control over
tenure-track faculty numbers. Administrations everywhere have put into
place stringent systems of "position control" that govern the numbers
of tenure-track faculty. These systems employ elaborate and time-
consuming authorization procedures that usually ensure that no new
tenure-track faculty member is hired unless another is committed to res-
ignation or retirement.

Authorization of new faculty "lines" is possible too, but that requires
new funds to be made available through special appropriations or new
endowments. For example, in 2007, the University of Michigan
announced a new program to add 100 interdisciplinary tenure-track
faculty members over five years and the University of Virginia pledged
to add 300 over ten years.[2] However, even if a central administrative
authority is persuaded to approve new lines, the intellectual areas for the
lines will usually be determined by faculty members on a committee or

by a dean who, at our elite research universities, is more powerfully driven by academic research and scholarly needs than by teaching needs. Even if teaching needs do generate a new line, they do not necessarily control its specific field. Most tenured faculty members appear to believe that they can teach beginning and intermediate-level classes in any subdiscipline within their fields. Few, however, believe that a specialist in Chinese history can do effective research on the French revolution. Thus, there is much more willingness to accept subdiscipline substitutions in the undergraduate classroom than in the research enterprise or the graduate program. As a result, the allocation of new faculty positions is much more heavily influenced by perceptions of research opportunities than by teaching needs.

In practice, teaching needs at distinguished research universities are not likely to extract budgetary support for new tenure-track faculty lines. Many administrators appear to fear that increased teaching needs are temporary in spite of sometimes long histories of enrollment growth. Moreover, there is always uncertainty regarding the fields in which students will enroll. Student course enrollments can shift dramatically from one year to the next—from political science to biology and then over to economics—in response to current events, the state of the economy, or exciting developments in the fields. Appointment of a new tenure-track faculty member introduces inflexibility in the face of this uncertainty. The appointment of non-tenure-track faculty is a much safer choice.

This is an area in which the behavior of the research-intensive universities in our study undoubtedly differs from that of regional, comprehensive, liberal arts, or (especially) for-profit institutions. New lines may well be approved in a research institution in response to the emergence of a new and important field of study. The need to keep up with a field is more compelling than is the need to add instructional staff because the latter can be met as well by other means. Institutions less concerned with research are more heavily influenced by teaching needs, and they therefore are more likely to hire in direct response to teaching pressures, but they are also likely to rely on untenured faculty who can be replaced when disciplinary teaching needs change.

The upshot of all this is that the numbers of tenure-track faculty have remained relatively constant over the last several decades. Among the ten institutions in our study, none increased its full-time equivalents (FTEs) of tenure-track faculty by more than 10 percent over the twenty-five-year period from 1980 to 2005. In contrast, most displayed a significant growth in undergraduate populations over the same period (in one case, over 70 percent). In an era of difficult budgets, central administrators in higher education have been reluctant to shoulder the long-term financial obligations that result from an increase in the numbers of tenure-track faculty; therefore, their numbers remain relatively fixed.[3] Because the number of graduate students is largely determined by the number of tenured and tenure-track faculty (who must shoulder the burdens of teaching and mentoring them), their numbers are also held relatively constant, except in engineering and the sciences, where they grow as research funding grows. That leaves non-tenure-track faculty as the only instructional category that can be readily increased.

In this sense, cost remains a driving force behind non-tenure-track appointments, even though each individual non-tenure-track appointment may take place initially for reasons other than cost. Our point is that resource-allocation decisions and appointment decisions are taking place at different levels, at different times, and for different reasons. The administrators who are concerned about controlling costs through control over tenure-track faculty positions are not the same people who actually hire the non-tenure-track instructors. Rarely is anyone in the hierarchy in a position to decide to use more of the less expensive of two substitutable resources. Indeed, except for the occasional economist, we rarely encountered anyone who could provide a plausible per-course cost comparison between instruction by tenure-track faculty and instruction by a graduate student or a lecturer, particularly because there is no reliable way to apportion tenure-track faculty salaries across the spectrum of faculty responsibilities.

At the institutional level, cost is a critical driver. At the department level, teaching and personnel issues are the critical drivers. The institution enforces rigidity in the numbers of tenure-stream faculty and graduate students, leaving non-tenure-track faculty as the only instructors who are available to serve increasing numbers of students. The growing demand for non-tenure-track instruction directly reflects the growing demand for postsecondary education and a budget-driven rigidity in the provision of alternatives.

The outcome is that expanding enrollment demand is met with non-tenure-track faculty. This process is not confined to the internal management of research institutions: it extends to the entire market for higher education. Although some of the nationwide increase in enrollment in institutions of higher education has occurred in places such as the ones we studied, the bulk of the increase has occurred in other settings—comprehensive colleges, two-year colleges, regional branches of public university systems, and most recently for-profit entities. Most of these new institutions do not build their curricula around tenure-track faculty. Many (such as for-profit colleges) do not hire any tenured faculty at all, and most others employ a high proportion of non-tenure-track faculty. Thus we see a larger-scale version of the adaptations that we have just described. It is difficult to secure increased financial support for an institution of higher education that uses a core of tenure-track faculty, and this limits the growth potential of such institutions. That constraint on growth creates a market niche for nontraditional institutions, which do not rely heavily on expensive teaching personnel. The national expansion in enrollments is served through the growth of less expensive institutions that use a much smaller proportion of tenure-track faculty. Although the proportion of total faculty FTE represented by non-tenure-track instructors in Association of American Universities (AAU) schools is estimated to be about 20 percent, the national proportion is much greater, with estimates ranging as high as 50 percent.[4]

Instructional Productivity Increases Rely on Non-Tenure-Track Faculty

Conventional wisdom holds that residential higher education does not lend itself to productivity gains from technology. Unlike manufacturing, where technological innovations have drastically decreased costs over the last century, few innovations economize on the human factors used in instruction. Advances in audiovisual presentation and the introduction of computers into instruction may have improved the *quality* of instruction but have not reduced the numbers of instructors who are necessary to provide it. If anything, they have increased the numbers of support staff who are needed to maintain the equipment. Especially in research universities, the basic model of instruction remains real-time interactions between faculty member and student, and this fact is often cited to explain increases in the cost of education relative to the cost of manufactured goods.

Certain devices can be used to economize on instructional resources and therefore improve the productivity of faculty. Policies that encourage students to take a term or year of study abroad relieve institutions of on-campus teaching requirements, and distance education purports to economize on traditional instructional resources by making instruction available online rather than in the classroom. Neither of these, however, significantly decreased instructional costs in the institutions in our study. Study-abroad programs have been in place for a long time, and even though international experiences for students are mentioned regularly as priorities by presidents of these institutions, growth in study-abroad enrollments has not kept up with growth in overall undergraduate enrollments. Similarly, we heard little mention of distance education in our interviews, probably because the students attending the universities in our study sample were predominantly residents rather than commuters.

Two main vehicles for productivity increases remain—increases in classes offered per instructor and increases in class size. As we have already indicated, more classes offered per instructor is possible if more NTT faculty are hired, each of whom teaches more classes per semester than a TT instructor. With regard to class size, when undergraduate enrollments grow at a faster rate than instructor availability, simple arithmetic demonstrates that the student-to-faculty ratio increases. It does not follow, however, that class formats are changing or that discussion classes are being replaced by lectures. A classroom that accommodated twenty students three decades ago will still accommodate twenty students now. Our interviews uncovered no evidence that older classrooms are being replaced by new, larger lecture halls. We did encounter pervasive efforts to use classes more efficiently. A class of eight students that is located in a room that will accommodate twenty students or a lecture of forty students that is located in a lecture hall with capacity for

100 is described as "underenrolled," and every university works hard to eliminate underenrolled classes.

We observed two strategies in use for reducing underenrolled classes. One is to set a minimum class size and enforce it by asking tenure-track faculty to offer low-enrollment courses only every other year. The other strategy relies heavily on the presence of non-tenure-track faculty. If two sections of a lower-division course are enrolling only eight students each, they can be collapsed into one section of sixteen, eliminating the need for one instructor. A classroom merger would not save money if a tenure-track instructor needs to be assigned elsewhere. However, the number of non-tenure-track instructors can be reduced. This is the basis of the derogatory term *contingent faculty*.

We have noted that the bulk of non-tenure-track teaching takes place in lower-division courses (those taken in the first and second years). The most common explanation for this (and one that we have already put forward) is that because tenure-track faculty members are much more interested in teaching upper-division and graduate courses than introductory courses, the lower-division courses are assigned to non-tenure-track faculty by default. This explanation remains valid. However, we now offer the additional observation that the productivity increases that come from combining sections apply only to courses taught in multiple parallel sections, which are found primarily in the lower division. Thus the productivity increase provided by non-tenure-track faculty occurs there as well.

Seeking Non-Tenure-Track Employment: The Supply Side

Faculty members on the tenure track face multiple responsibilities—teaching, generating cutting-edge research, performing university service, and mentoring graduate students. In combination, these obligations can lead to heavy workloads that require work on weekends and during the long vacation periods enjoyed by students and instructors whose responsibilities are limited to teaching alone.[5]

Even with greater formal teaching loads, the time commitments of non-tenure-track faculty are often smaller than those of research-active, tenure-track faculty.[6] Nevertheless, the literature on non-tenure-track faculty tends to focus exclusively on teaching efforts, and non-tenure-track positions usually have heavier teaching loads than tenured positions. Moreover, compared with tenure-track employment, non-tenure-track positions have many disadvantages—significantly lower salary, fewer benefits, lack of job security, less control over teaching assignments, inferior office support, and lower status. News accounts of this situation, which use loaded terms such as *contingent* or *exploited* faculty, lead some to wonder why anyone is willing to enter the market and provide these services in the first place.

Men and women who have achieved a PhD or MA degree have acquired professional skills that would surely qualify them for positions outside of academia. The occasional claim that prospective graduate students are foolishly unaware of their limited prospects in the tenured academic market is no longer credible. Negative publicity about employment opportunities in certain fields is extensive, and acceptance letters to graduate programs and recruitment visits often convey warnings about the lack of tenure-track career prospects in some fields or subfields. Yet students continue to apply for PhD programs, complete their studies, and accept non-tenure-track employment.

Several factors lead to continued participation in this market, three of which appear to us to be most salient.

Job Satisfaction

Surveys of non-tenure-track faculty do not uncover low morale or job dissatisfaction. Indeed, the levels of some aspects of job satisfaction appear to be comparable to or even higher than those expressed by tenured faculty.[7] One consistently reported source of dissatisfaction is the lack of long-term job security, but even this result is hard to interpret. It could reflect a desire for greater job security without any changes in job duties (a benefit with no corresponding costs), or it could reflect a preference for a position that carried the full range of tenured faculty benefits and responsibilities (a preference for a different job).

Existing surveys and descriptions of non-tenure-track circumstances do not distinguish between these two alternatives. Surveys ask questions that use "teaching load" as the only metric for comparison, leaving out anything related to service, research, or graduate student mentoring. Instructors without tenure inevitably express their preference for more job security because survey questions imply that it would come without a cost. If surveys asked non-tenure-track instructors if they would prefer to be on the tenure track, commit vacation time and weekends to research, undergo stressful promotion reviews (with their potential for failure and termination), perform university service, and mentor graduate students, the instructors' responses might be different.

Ironically, job security for new assistant professors on a tenure track may not be higher than that for non-tenure-track instructors. For the institutions in our study, the success rate for tenure is 75 percent or less, and when we include those who leave before a tenure decision is made (sometimes in anticipation of a negative decision), the success rate drops to 50 percent or less. It is not unusual for non-tenure-track instructors who are offered tenure-track positions to decline the opportunity, either because the institution that offers the position is in a different geographical region (and may not be regarded as equivalent in quality), because the work expectations are too great, or because termination (through failure to achieve tenure) is a real possibility.

This is far from the whole answer, however. Different institutions offer different employment packages to non-tenure-track instructors, and until we address that question (later in this chapter), we cannot form general conclusions. Nevertheless, we do have a part of the answer to the original question: PhD holders accept these positions rather than pursuing non-academic careers because they prefer these jobs to those alternatives. Even if they would prefer positions that offer more benefits, it does not follow that they wish they had chosen some other career.

Part-time and Adjunct Instructors

Many part-time instructors are hired because they bring experience and skills to the campus that would be unavailable from full-time academic staff. Just as a curriculum is enriched through the presence of individuals whose careers are firmly grounded outside of academia, so too those individuals often feel enriched by interacting with students and engaging in academic reflections on their own careers. Artists of all types fit into this designation, but it applies as well to engineers, mathematicians, social scientists, business executives, and scientists whose careers have remained largely in private enterprise or government. In some fields—especially those whose income prospects are irregular—there is a financial motive as well. Visual artists and musicians frequently seek out part-time positions because they offer a level of financial stability in an otherwise uncertain world.

We have already noted that one reason that the use of part-time instructors is growing is because the recent expansion in enrollments is not an expansion of a homogeneous student body but rather an expansion beyond the boundaries of the traditional student clientele. The contemporary emphasis on attracting diverse student bodies means that universities are enrolling more and more students with acknowledged preprofessional career aspirations.[8] These students are not replicas of students from decades ago. All of the universities in our study acknowledge a broader array of student interests, and although none is abandoning or reducing its commitment to the liberal arts, almost all are meeting those additional interests with practitioners rather than with academics whose backgrounds are placed entirely within the academic sphere.

In this case, the answer to our fundamental supply question is self-evident. Part-time adjunct faculty members accept positions at elite research universities because they find them to be personally rewarding. They already have alternative careers, and if they choose part-time academic employment, they see it to be in their own interests. Artists may want some income stability, but they do not seek full-time employment that leaves little time for their art.

Risk and Uncertainty

This is the most subtle of our three reasons for the willing supply of PhD recipients to non-tenure-track ranks, but it may be the most important. The statistical career prospects for an entering graduate student in any field are well known (or at least easily obtained). Many students who enter graduate programs will not find regular tenure-track academic employment. In some fields, a third or more will drop out without completing a PhD, and many of those with PhDs will either take positions outside of academia or will follow careers as non-tenure-track instructors. (In some of the sciences as well as engineering, employment in the private sector may be the preferred career choice anyway.) The statistical likelihood that a student who first enters graduate school will end up in a tenured position in an elite research university is low—a fact that is now universally recognized. By now, the market situation in many disciplines is well known, and although the dropout rate for graduate students is poorly publicized, it can be easily uncovered by any prospective graduate student before matriculation.

Throughout the 1990s, the tightness of the academic market in the humanities was widely publicized, and yet the number of students entering programs in the humanities grew. Over the same period, a number of departments warned prospective students about their poor career prospects, but these warnings did not appear to reduce enrollments. Perhaps these students believed that they would not themselves be the ones to fail to find employment.

The explanation that appeals to us is derived from the economic theory of risk taking. As an example, consider the situation of a prospective student who would prefer a tenure-track academic position, with all its inherent costs and benefits, to that of any alternative career. (Whether the alternative is a non-tenure-track teaching position or something else is not material.) Knowing that some fraction of graduate students will end up in non-tenure-track careers is not the same as knowing exactly what one's own career path will be, but failure to obtain a tenure-track position has to be accepted as a possibility. Entering graduate school is thus like entering a lottery in which a win is a tenure-track (and ultimately tenured) position and a loss is some alternative career.

Those who purchase state lottery tickets do so in hopes of winning the grand prize. For nearly everyone, that hope is not fulfilled, but for most, the loss (the cost of the tickets) is not a disaster. For graduate students who do not ultimately obtain tenured positions, the loss is the time and expense of obtaining the graduate education and the acceptance of employment that is not their first choice, but their loss, too, is not a disaster. It leads to an alternative career with rewards of its own. Is it any wonder that a lottery whose prize is a high-prestige and (reasonably) well-paid academic position and whose default is a sustainable career will tend to attract large numbers of applicants?[9]

In this respect, pursuit of an academic career is like the pursuit of any other career that may lead to varying degrees of success. Almost every professional career generates a dispersion of salary and prestige among its participants. Historically (at least in the mythology), academic careers have been more or less uniformly compensated, but the dispersion in outcomes for academic careers has increased dramatically in recent years. Academic careers were much less uncertain before the emergence of non-tenure-track faculty positions and before the institution of differential salary increases within tenured-faculty ranks. The security of academic jobs and their relatively horizontal salary structures were often cited as benefits—and also as explanations for their fairly low salaries. Faculty members were often described as individuals who had stepped away from the competitiveness and uncertainty of the commercial world, having chosen instead the secure, though modest, income offered by a lifetime commitment to teaching.

In recent decades, status and financial compensation across academia have substantially diverged. The highest-paid faculty members are paid extraordinarily well, sometimes as much as ten times the salary of the lowest-paid full-time instructor.[10] The active research biologist teaches part of a course each year, while the full-time lecturer in English teaches three courses a term. In effect, PhDs today are entering a lottery where no lottery existed before. Those who do not reap the greatest gains from this lottery are understandably disappointed with the outcome, even though it does not threaten their survival.

We do not believe that academic culture has abandoned entirely the assumptions of egalitarianism that have long held sway. Indeed, we suspect that the dissonance between what those ideals are and what is actually occurring in the academic marketplace is partially responsible for the hostile rhetoric that is found in most of the writing on the question of non-tenure-track instruction. Nevertheless, we are convinced that even without the uniformity in compensation and job responsibility that may have prevailed in the past, the mix of potential outcomes is still sufficient to attract individuals into the teaching profession.

Other Factors in the Market for Non-Tenure-Track Employment

We designed a study of universities that looked at several geographic and financial features because we expected that the economic environment would affect the terms under which universities employ instructors. We included institutions that differ with respect to geography (city versus country), funding sources (public versus private), and internal budgeting systems. We discuss budget systems in chapter 6, but first we turn to geography and funding sources below.

Geography

Non-tenure-track instructors usually come from local populations. University officials frequently speak of carrying out national searches for non-tenure-track positions, just as they do for tenure-track faculty, but the reality falls far short of this ideal. Most are unwilling to devote the time and resources necessary for a national search for these positions, and by default, they turn to individuals who are already at hand—former graduate students of their own or nearby universities, partners of university staff, or other individuals who live near the school. This means that the market for non-tenure-track faculty is a local or regional market and that the terms of employment are likely to reflect local or regional conditions.

A striking disparity exists between urban and nonurban pay rates for non-tenure-track academic instruction. Urban areas (including suburbs) have large numbers of persons with advanced degrees and academic teaching skills who are willing (sometimes eager) to take on part-time or even full-time NTT positions for modest salaries. In contrast, less populated areas do not have large numbers of practitioners in the arts, sciences, or business who can conveniently devote a day or an evening to teaching. A relatively thin professional market is less likely to include partners of local professionals who would be suitable for an occasional teaching assignment, although academic partners sometimes have few choices other than an NTT appointment. As a result, NTT salaries in nonurban settings are higher than they are in urban areas—unlike tenure-track faculty salaries, which are higher in urban areas with high costs of living. This means that differences in salaries of TT and NTT faculty are much greater in urban settings.

Some evidence suggests that this disparity is reflected in turnover rates as well. Turnover in non-tenure-track positions is in part an outcome of university policies. Before the increase in numbers of non-tenure-track instructors, many universities followed policies that limited the number of reappointment contracts for non-tenure-track staff. Almost all appointments were year by year (or even semester by semester), and renewal beyond a certain period (three or six years typically) was frowned on or even forbidden. The American Association of University Professors (AAUP) often cited a seven-year rule for all full-time faculty positions, whether tenure-track or not. Except for "special appointments clearly limited to a brief association with the institution ... non-tenure track appointments do considerable damage both to principles of academic freedom and tenure and to the quality of our academic institutions—not to mention the adverse consequences for the individuals serving in such appointments."[11]

These limits to appointment longevity have been breaking down almost everywhere. The standard one-year appointment is being replaced by systems of multiyear appointments, and the stringent limits on the numbers of reappointments are also being dropped. These changes are appearing most rapidly outside of urban markets, while the holdouts are found in urban areas. In less populated areas, replacement of the specialists that are required for instruction is especially difficult, whereas adhering to the traditional rules is easier in urban areas, which have substantial numbers of qualified people to replace those who have exhausted policy limits.

Public versus Private

Elite private universities have much higher endowments per student and charge more tuition than public universities. The impression of affluence is reinforced by media attention to a few well-endowed private universities and to their high endowment investment returns. The gap between the wealthiest private and public universities is growing quickly, as endowments have been growing much faster than state contributions (which in some places have actually been shrinking). Despite this, observations that all privates have more discretionary money to support undergraduate instruction are easy to exaggerate:

• Most private institutions have limited resources that are available for instruction. Despite the publicity given to those with huge endowments, many private university endowments are modest, and even those with large endowments face restrictions on how income can be used. The largest share of a university endowment represents gifts that have been earmarked by donors for specific purposes, such as research institutes, individual professorships, scholarships, or buildings. Attempts to bypass these restrictions are almost certain to invite lawsuits.[12] Because of this earmarking, a large endowment enhances the research reputations of a university and its capacity to attract the most promising faculty and students, but it does not necessarily do much to support regular undergraduate teaching.

• The relatively stable flow of state funds to public universities is often equivalent to the income that can be obtained from a substantial endowment. A large state university that receives $100 million annually from its legislature is receiving the equivalent of the income from an endowment of $2 billion dollars, more or less, which would put it among the best-endowed of all private universities. More important, that income is largely not earmarked and can be spent on general operations. That absence of earmarking enables public universities to compete for tenured faculty at the same time that they can offer tuition below that of most private universities and enroll substantially larger numbers of students.

• Many states support higher education facilities through state bonds that are not available to private universities. This resource commitment supplements the direct money that states provide. It also means that the facilities of public universities are at least as modern and attractive as those offered by private institutions noted for their endowment wealth. Occasionally, states use this bonding authority as a countercyclical policy tool, expanding building activity during times when other sectors of the economy are weak, to the envy of private institutions.

Location is an important factor in faculty job choices.[13] With location and overall job expectations fairly constant, association with a high-prestige department appeals to instructors.[14] Given a choice of institutions, we would expect a part-time teacher to choose the one that was more highly ranked and that therefore might offer the most committed and interesting students, the most stimulating intellectual environment, and the most status associated with name recognition. One might expect this preference to be revealed by a willingness to accept a lower salary than is paid by less prestigious institutions in the same geographical area. In fact, the reverse appears to be the case. In the cases that came to our attention, compensation was significantly more generous overall in the high-prestige institutions in our study than in other universities in the same areas, even if it was higher in less populated locations than in urban centers.

Finally, we chose some universities that had adopted new budgetary systems and some that had not because we had observed the impact of responsibility-centered management on instructional decisions at Michigan. We turn to this topic in the next chapter.

6

The Invasion of the Business Models

The decline in legislative support for public higher education became apparent as early as the 1970s. University administrators routinely attributed this decline to the increased demands from competing publicly supported enterprises (such as public K–12 education, Medicaid payments, and corrections) rather than to a loss of prestige or respect for their own institutions. By the late 1980s, however, evidence was accumulating that the public was increasingly unhappy with the performance of higher education.[1] Much of this unhappiness had economic roots: over the last three decades, tuition costs have grown much faster than family incomes, consumer prices in general, or student financial aid, so that students now graduate with debts that are dramatically higher than those of students from earlier generations.

Media reports of tuition increases are occasionally supplemented by stories of university malfeasance (exorbitant senior administrator salaries, misrepresentation of research, and mismanaged student crises) or of huge and rapidly growing university endowments. These events have reinforced a general public view that universities, public and private, are plagued by a self-satisfied inefficiency that imposes inappropriate costs on students, their parents, and the general public. Even trustees of these institutions sometimes share in this view.

A common response that is advocated by college and university trustees with business backgrounds has been to call for the application of business techniques to higher education. These pressures reflect two widely accepted stereotypes: one of efficient, goal-oriented business leaders who get the job done and yet manage costs effectively, and another of tweed-jacketed pipe-smoking academic administrators who have no business training, have never met a payroll, and are not particularly concerned with how the finances of their institutions work.

These stereotypes credit the business community with considerably more competence and the academic community with less competence than experience warrants. Nevertheless, these views have led to calls for greater accountability by universities, both public and private. In 2006, the U.S. Department of Education's review of higher education (the Spellings Commission) produced a report that expresses barely muted hostility toward nonprofit educational institutions and affirms private-sector management ideals and principles.[2] Governors, state legislators, and members of the U.S. Congress contribute to this general tone by challenging large tuition increases and questioning the large size and low payouts of endowments.

Long before the Spellings Commission, many colleges and universities had reviewed their internal financing structures, and some developed business models that promised to deal with financial pressures. In doing so, university presidents and provosts tried to mollify the corporate members of their boards of trustees and convince donors and the public that higher education deserves their support and respect.[3]

Opportunities for productive expenditures always exceed the resources available in higher education. Administrators at top-tier research-active universities are under constant pressure to deal with competing demands for support. This pressure appears to be increasing: declining state support (for public institutions) together with rising fuel and health care costs, the costs of recruiting students and increasing federal requirements (for all institutions) contribute to budget stringency.

Less obvious is the role that is played by faculty in resource allocation. Those outside the university environment usually underestimate the influence of tenure-track faculty on university decision making and overestimate the ability of administrators to control costs. The power of the faculty is often invisible from the outside, perhaps because it is rarely challenged in public. This authority rests on two main factors. First, the national and international standing of a research-active university is virtually synonymous with the national and international standing of its faculty. In chapter 4, we described the fierce competition among leading universities for the best faculty, and that competition conveys influence to the faculty members themselves. An administrator who takes actions that antagonize prominent faculty members endangers the reputation of the institution and, consequently, the security of his or her own future.

Second, the harsh reality of administrative life in a research-competitive environment is that administrators have such heavy demands on their time that they have difficulty maintaining their research careers. This is especially true for presidents, provosts, and deans of arts and sciences. To rejoin a faculty in a teaching and research role is challenging. After five or more years, one can rarely recover research momentum and regain one's former stature in a fast-moving academic field.

In effect, accepting a senior administrative position usually amounts to a permanent career change, and the two options in that new career are either longevity in the current role or a position at a higher administrative level, usually somewhere else. It is a rare dean who does not consider becoming a provost and a rare provost who does not hope to become a university president. However, elite universities are reluctant to hire or even retain administrators who have acquired reputations for antagonizing the faculty or triggering departures of academic stars, and this simple fact of life gives tenure-track faculty enormous influence. It is no surprise that university presidents have become bland in their public statements and that many of them have lost the outspoken social leadership styles that used to characterize the role.

Faculty members are willing to exploit their advantages with the administration, and they are adept at doing so. Most faculty members are highly articulate, having gained experience in the arts of persuasion through years of proposal writing and classroom activity. Moreover, they know how to exploit their membership in highly visible academic associations. A dean seeking to reduce or eliminate funding for an established program must be willing to face an outpouring of opposition—from faculty, students, alumni, representatives of the discipline at other institutions, the press, and even political figures. He or she will experience public protests, photographs in the media, testimonials from former students, letters to the editor, and contentious faculty meetings. Details of the resulting "dispute" will appear in the *Chronicle of Higher Education* and in the education sections of national newspapers.[4] By the end of the process, even if the change is made successfully, the fate of that dean may be sealed. This kind of highly publicized resistance to change is virtually unknown in private commercial settings, where any such discussions would take place internally in a context of priority-setting or program substitution.

This political reality carries a financial consequence. Presidents, provosts, and deans on elite campuses rarely challenge their faculty directly, and by extension, they rarely challenge the continued existence of long-standing programs, whatever their cost and their relevance to contemporary curricular needs. The only remaining mechanism for change is growth—using new resources to support new and popular initiatives at the same time that the old programs remain in place. New and exciting programs are launched, but old programs are rarely eliminated, and overall costs rise.

Many outside the academic community believe that this underlying rigidity in resource allocation is attributable to the institution of tenure, which might limit the elimination of low-priority teaching resources. In our opinion, tenure is not the central issue. Almost all college and university by-laws restrict tenure, in one way or another, to a department or program. They do not guarantee continued employment if the underlying need for instruction goes away. Tenure will certainly protect the occasional faculty member who is simply a pain in the neck or who expresses controversial political views, but it does not offer comparable protection to someone with no students to teach. Even so, prestigious universities go to great lengths to avoid terminating faculty members with tenure. They encourage them to teach in other areas if enrollments drop or provide financial sweeteners to encourage early retirement. Leaders of prestigious universities do not want a reputation for firing tenured faculty members, but those faculty members can be shifted from one program to another. The rigidity that sustains existing intellectual areas even as new ones are added stems instead from the nature of the professoriate itself—the easy mobility of internationally recognized faculty members and their capacity to transform themselves into enormously articulate defenders of the status quo. The stronger the international reputations of faculty, the more difficult it is for administrators to reallocate resources.

Incremental Budgeting

This political environment affects costs and shapes the budgeting process itself. It produces a model under which all departments receive their proportionate share of any general financial increase, while new initiatives are supported through incremental resources or from small allotments reserved from the general budget. This in turn leads to budgetary concepts that are not found in business settings, such as the notion of a "fair distribution of resources"—a concept that arises almost routinely in academic budget discussions. People with business backgrounds find this entitlement inconceivable: it is as though each division of a large automobile manufacturer expected to maintain its share of corporate resources regardless of productivity or sales. The incremental model must appear anachronistic to anyone unfamiliar with academe because the underlying faculty influence that has brought it about is often invisible to anyone outside the system.

Under incremental budgeting, revenues (chiefly composed of tuition revenue, state allocations for publics, indirect cost revenue, and endowment income) are assigned to a central administration; costs are divided into two types—central service costs (library, health service, administrative salaries, and the like), which are to be covered from central funds, and unit costs (instructional salaries, staff salaries, teaching supplies, and sometimes space and maintenance), which are assigned to colleges and departments and which are covered by appropriations from the general pool of resources. Although the highest administrators of the university have authority over the distribution of resources to the schools and colleges, in reality, the pattern of financial allocations changes very little over time. If university revenues grow from one year to the next by 4 percent (through an increase in enrollment, in tuition, or in state appropriations), the baseline expectation of each department or unit is that the central administration will award an increase of close to 4 percent, permitting all units to share more or less equally in the revenue growth. This is the sense of a "fair" distribution of resources. Endowment income and private giving are either specified for use or available for discretionary purposes and generally independent of the "fair" distribution.

Any mechanical resource allocation system can be exploited, and the incremental budgeting process is no exception. Under incremental budgeting, a unit might abandon or reduce a program without facing significant adverse financial consequences, even though the contraction diminishes the revenue stream to the institution as a whole. On the other hand, if the same unit proposes a new program that will attract new students, unit leaders will describe it as a new initiative and point to the associated costs as the basis for an increased claim on central resources. Indeed, the unit might refuse to implement a valuable new program unless it is assured that the central administration will provide incremental support.

Putting these two together, a good strategy for increasing the resources available to a semi-independent school or college is to cut one program (suffering no loss of revenues) while expanding another (supported by incremental resources). Put as baldly as this, those outside the university might well be astonished that such a transparent strategy for increasing a unit's share of university resources might work—but it has worked, many times over. Essentially, it exploits the political dynamic embedded in the governance structure of higher education at the nation's leading universities—a structure that produces administrators who are reluctant to incur the wrath of faculty and unit deans. Many observers believe that the inefficient incentive structure embodied in incremental budgeting has been responsible for the apparently unstoppable escalation of costs and for the growing disparity between the high charges levied on students and the relatively smaller costs of educating some of them, particularly those in the liberal arts colleges.

Responsibility-Centered Management (RCM)

The deficiencies of incremental budgeting have led to proposals for strengthening the financial links between revenues and performance. The most prominent among them is responsibility-centered management (RCM)—a strategy that treats the many components of a large multiunit organization as though they were separate businesses that operate within their own individual markets, with their own identifiable revenue streams and their own identifiable costs. Underlying these schemes is an assumption that once academic units are given their own bottom-line structures, the magic of the market will force them to improve performance on both the cost and the revenue sides.[5]

In its most literal form, RCM directs revenues to each unit in proportion to the tuition payments made by its students, and costs of instruction are covered from those same revenues. Such a strategy removes incentives to close programs without regard for the lost revenues and to create new programs without securing the income to support them. When it was first proposed, responsibility-centered management appeared to be an ideal antidote to the passive funding properties of incremental budgeting because it promised to introduce a significant level of financial discipline into academic decision making.

Indeed, RCM did facilitate long-term planning by allowing academic units to retain unspent balances. Prior to RCM, academic units were usually obliged to return unspent balances to the dean or provost. To avoid doing that, these units often engaged in last-minute (and sometimes wasteful) spending sprees. Units could have been permitted to carry over unspent balances under a system of incremental budgeting, but it usually took RCM-like thinking to clarify why this would be a good practice.

Unfortunately, RCM's promise has not been fulfilled. The main reasons are four:

• RCM and its descendants ignore the political dynamic that created incremental budgeting in the first place. The premise of RCM is that incremental budgeting is the *cause* of the problem when in fact it is a *consequence* of the culture of higher education.

• Business models tend to oversimplify the academic mission, reducing a rich diversity of purposes and goals into a single bottom line that is unacceptable to faculty members.

• Most RCM models ignore the complexity of the highly interdependent set of colleges and programs that characterize a research institution.

• RCM provides no mechanism for dealing with overhead allocation issues, which in turn leads to an incomplete cost-attribution model.

All these issues are important, and they are described more completely in the appendix to this chapter. The central issue for us in the context of our study is that these business models create powerful incentives to hire non-tenure-track faculty. The problems listed above all tend to drive the institution in that direction. This is primarily because NTT faculty are relatively inexpensive, and tuition charges are rarely linked to the costs of instruction. The enhanced profit motive that is embedded in the RCM bottom line reinforces any already present incentives to use expensive tenure-track faculty for other things and use inexpensive NTT faculty to do as much (revenue-generating) teaching as possible.

Moreover, by narrowing the mission focus, these systems lead to a narrower set of necessary qualifications of the teaching staff. They do not reward research (except for funded research with full overhead), intellectual diversity, improvement in the quality of education, or participation in less career-centered disciplines. If the university designs an incentive system for its academic mission that focuses primarily on classroom contact hours, why hire expensive tenure-track faculty when NTT faculty can do the job?[6]

Because RCM-inspired business models tend to shift administrative responsibilities down the hierarchy, they place temporary or rotating employment decisions in the hands of individuals who are least able to resist self-interested pressures from tenure-track faculty. Moreover, moving down the hierarchy, individuals are inevitably more distant from the values and objectives of senior administrators. Even when a provost or president is strongly opposed to the increased use of NTT faculty, this value may not extend to the individuals who make the actual hiring decisions. Indeed, they may not even be aware of policies to avoid increasing the reliance on NTT faculty.

RCM, like incremental budgeting, is a mechanical budgeting system, and it too can be exploited. One of the best devices for exploiting the vulnerabilities of RCM budget systems is to increase the use of NTT faculty. The procedure is straightforward: a professional school that has historically relied on a liberal arts college to offer elementary mathematics, writing, or science courses can choose to teach those courses within its own curriculum using inexpensive NTT faculty. This strategy will always be profitable because it will divert tuition income to the professional school on an average tuition-per-credit-hour basis, while meeting the additional teaching responsibility with the lowest-cost instructional resources. Profitable as it certainly is, this device compromises the traditional organization of a university around disciplinary cores. The faculty who are hired for these purposes usually come from disciplines that have no place in the professional school in question. For example, humanities requirements in engineering colleges may be met through the use of PhDs in fields that would otherwise never be found in an engineering school. These instructors cannot join in the intellectual fabric of the school in which they are hired to teach. The school values them primarily as hired hands who teach specific subjects and has no concern for their scholarly interests or professional development.

Narrowing the Mission

Responsibility-centered management is only one example of the *corporatization* of higher education.[7] Business models tend to narrow the mission focus of a university by reinforcing a relatively narrow set of outcomes. Virtually any model that is borrowed from the private sector will have the same consequence. University interest in RCM and its variants is gradually fading, but the dominant theme of outcome-based funding is not. Advocacy for the use of quantifiable outcome measures is appearing in both legislative and accreditation venues. There is much talk of retention and graduation rates, learning outcomes, access for lower-income students, postgraduation outcomes, and academic achievement. These outcomes are worthy of concern, and they lend themselves to quantification. However, they do not capture the entire range of purposes that most universities define for themselves. Instead, they embody a kind of "filling station" model of higher education: the driver coasts to the pump with an empty gas tank, pays money, and drives away with a gas gauge that says "full."

This conception of education imagines that students enter college knowing little, pay tuition and fees, and depart knowing more. This is a part of what happens, but most participants in higher education expect much more. University faculty strive to help students know what they do not know, which questions to ask, how to make and analyze arguments, how to assess the credibility of evidence and sources, and so on. They try to instill in their students a love of learning, a healthy skepticism toward unsubstantiated claims, an appreciation for other cultures and perspectives, and a commitment to continuing to learn for the rest of their lives. These objectives are not easily measured and are rarely included in outcome measures that can capture only the educational equivalent of the gas gauge. A focus on readily measurable goals necessarily contributes to a narrowing of the mission of higher education.

Pressures to measure the achievement of educational goals in the public sector may be widening the gap between public and private universities. Private universities depend for their support on student enrollment and alumni support, which in turn depend on instruction as well as less readily defined factors, such as institutional prestige, quality of life on campus, networking, and social experiences. Private institutions attract their support through their ability to articulate a broad agenda. This is the traditional framework in which universities have differentiated themselves, and the strategy still works well. In contrast, public support for higher education is rapidly moving away from prestige and personal rewards toward quantifiable outcome measures such as high SAT scores or graduation rates. As those goals become more closely linked to the teaching enterprise, NTT faculty, whose primary responsibility is teaching ("to fill the tank," so to speak) acquire an increasingly important role. Over the long run, we expect these forces to support the expansion of NTT faculty in public institutions. Non-tenure-track faculty are hired to teach, and teaching outcomes are now at the center of attention in public funding debates.

Regional accreditation agencies will not likely check this growth. They used to require a high proportion of tenure-track faculty for accreditation, but their willingness to award accreditation to for-profit colleges that employ no tenure-track faculty suggests that support for traditional tenure-track faculty and their value systems is losing its grip on the very organizations that are expected to serve as watchdogs over the entire higher educational enterprise.

Business models, legislative pressures, and simple budget stringency all create powerful incentives to hire non-tenure-track faculty. At the same time, universities are not institutions that respond rapidly to changes in financial incentives. A former dean from an institution that embraced responsibility-centered management suggested to us that reactions to new financial incentives are closely linked to turnover in administration.

He has observed that the initial reaction to a new business model is minor because department chairs and deans interpret the new system as simply an accounting change and people with academic backgrounds are not likely to view changes in accounting as a reason to change operations. However, new chairs and deans try to put their own stamps on their institutions by looking for new financial opportunities, and business models give them new opportunities—particularly through the employment of non-tenure-track faculty. The changes that they bring about may appear to be linked to other factors and not to the business models themselves. This is not a hypothesis that is readily tested in a short-term study such as ours, but it is born from experience and worth considering.

The Financial Ratchet

In an era of budget constraints and intense competition among institutions, benign motives for hiring non-tenure-track faculty can lead to a trap. NTT faculty *are* less expensive than tenured faculty, and once an instructor ineligible for tenure is hired instead of someone on the tenure track, university financial resources are aligned accordingly (that is, the unspent funds are used for something else). A subsequent decision to replace that NTT faculty member with someone on the tenure-track would require more money—a significant redirection of funds away from other uses or an infusion of new funds. If the NTT incumbent of the position is reasonably successful, tight budgets will work to maintain the status quo, and the new NTT position will become a fixture.

For the same reason, when a NTT faculty member leaves, he or she is likely to be replaced by another NTT faculty member, even if the replacement individual falls into an entirely different subfield. A department that wishes to encourage a senior faculty member to retire may offer a retirement package that includes the opportunity to teach one or two courses. When that faculty member eventually retires and stops teaching, the resulting teaching shortfall will almost certainly be filled by an adjunct or some other category of NTT faculty—if it is filled at all. Thus the initial motivation for using nontenured instruction has vanished, but the phenomenon of non-tenure-track instruction has remained in place.

This is a simple, unidirectional ratchet. A non-tenure-track faculty member may be hired for any of a long list of good reasons. However, when that instructor's lower cost is integrated into the institutional budget, it becomes financially difficult to replace him or her with a tenure-track instructor. Such a system inexorably moves toward greater and greater use of NTT faculty, absent a substantial infusion of additional funds. This does not mean that regular TT faculty will go away or even be reduced in numbers. Indeed, we are convinced that will not happen. But expansion in instruction is most often supported by NTT resources, and the proportions of NTT faculty grow over time, just as the data indicate.

Our interviews confirm that whether or not financial pressures are responsible for the employment of NTT faculty, financial pressures preserve those positions once they are created. There are many sound academic reasons for hiring NTT faculty, but whatever the reason for the hiring, the NTT appointment costs less than the appointment of a tenure-track faculty member, and once the budget has been aligned to take advantage of those released resources, a new configuration is in place. The tendency toward rigidity now applies to those newly supported high-priority objectives, and a proposal to drop those new programs or expenses will meet the same vociferous objections that would apply to eliminating any other expense. Replacement of the NTT with TT faculty members becomes difficult, not because an administrator consciously chooses to increase their presence but because economic realignment has made restoration expensive.

This kind of ratchet mechanism applies even in institutions whose leaders openly oppose growth in employment of non-tenure-track instructors. In fact, most administrators in research institutions prefer TT to NTT hiring. However, once the NTT appointments have been made (for other reasons), there are plenty of financial and institutional reasons for keeping them there.

Our point is that when a financing system creates incentives in support of some set of outcomes, administrators do not need consciously to exploit those incentives for them to affect hiring. Economic necessity in the presence of a fluctuating environment is sufficient. We have noted that university administrators appear to be unaware of the employment patterns that are developing in their own institutions. We believe that this lack of awareness is due largely to this financial ratchet. Administrators do not think of NTT faculty as having increased in numbers for budgetary reasons because they did not hire NTT faculty for budgetary reasons. Ultimately, they may be retained for budgetary reasons, but by the time that reality sets in, the NTT faculty members are a part of the fabric of the institution, and to retain them does not have the appearance of a decision. Indeed, it may look more like a decision not to retain them. Someone who never decided to hire NTT faculty but who only preserved a status quo might easily think that there must not be a large number of teaching faculty ineligible for tenure. The operating decisions all had to do with something else.

Appendix 6A. Notes on Responsibility-Centered Management

A number of business-oriented practices have been urged on institutions of higher education, and responsibility-centered management is only one of them. The issues that arise with RCM are likely to apply to several business practices, and it is worthwhile then to review RCM as an exemplar. Provosts at a number of universities in our study rejected RCM as a potential financing model for their institutions. One provost visited another campus to see how RCM was working and summarized his decision by saying, "Our budget is centralized. . . . My university abhors complicated financial schemes that compensate colleges for traffic from other colleges. Money should not be an issue. Students should be able to take courses wherever they want." Responsibility-centered management is generally rejected for reasons of political realities, mission, interdependence, and complex overhead.

Political Realities

Like most business models, responsibility-centered management ignores the political dynamic that created incremental budgeting in the first place. Advocates of RCM appear to believe that a poorly designed budgeting system created managerial inefficiency and that its replacement with a bottom-line system will eliminate inefficiency. The causality, however, goes in the other direction: incremental budgeting is an outcome of the political and economic environment of the university, not the source of it. A different budget model in no way diminishes the power of tenure-track faculty to influence resource allocation. Indeed, it may make the problem worse.

The decentralization inherent in RCM tends to drive administrative responsibility further down the line, placing it in the hands of departmental administrators who are more vulnerable than senior administrators are to faculty pressures. Because of their senior administrative status, provosts and presidents have established some distance between themselves and the faculty, but the same is not true for department chairs and some deans. Most department chairs expect to rejoin the faculty at the end of their terms. They regard faculty as colleagues and friends. In addition, they face the possibility of role reversal: no department chair looks forward to rejoining a regular faculty in which a colleague who is unhappy with an earlier decision has become the next chair. Conservatism in resource allocation is even more prevalent at this level than it is in the president's office.

Mission

The apparent conservatism of the faculty is not entirely misplaced. Major universities are complex institutions with multiple goals and ideals. It is impossible to capture the richness and diversity of these ideals in a financial system, which, by its very nature, must compress all matters into a few summary numbers. To faculty, who ultimately are responsible for the academic mission of the institution, such summations give every appearance of oversimplification and are readily rejected as invalid indicators of institutional performance. If there is any single factor that leads participants in the academic enterprise to reject the relevance of business models in general, it is this difference between an overriding single-dimensioned outcome index typical of business (for example, return on investment) and the medley of ideals, objectives, goals, and principles that characterize a modern research university.

Participants in the private business sector of our economy also have multiple goals, but for them the financial summary embodied in a profit and loss statement is the dominant driver. The same is true of for-profit colleges, and this reduction of educational objectives to a single bottom line is one factor that makes participants in research universities often dismiss for-profit colleges and universities as unsuitable participants in the enterprise of higher education.

RCM budget models share in the propensity to oversimplify the educational mission. The primary metric used to govern resource allocation is teaching—sometimes reduced to nothing more than elemental credit-hour generation. Placing primary responsibility for funding on such a model suggests that credit-hour generation is the only valid use for tuition payments from students. No modern university would acknowledge instruction to be its only function. Administrators and faculty alike describe the missions of their institutions in broad terms. Teaching is certainly at the core, but the mission of higher education goes well beyond direct instruction to include the protection and preservation of intellectual history (via libraries and the teaching of classical courses), the development of new ideas and insights (advancement not just in the sciences but in the social sciences and the humanities as well) even in areas that may be temporarily out of fashion, and the fostering of discourse (even to the extent of encouraging debates on matters of both fact and policy).

Most faculty believe that society is better off as a consequence of these multiple goals. For example, before September 11, 2001, *Afghanistanism* was a term reserved for hopelessly arcane and irrelevant scholarship. Today, knowledge of Afghanistan is highly valued. Achievement of many of the goals of leading universities does not generate tuition in any significant sense, and most faculty recognize that an RCM system would challenge many of the core values that they associate with university life. At the University of Michigan, the adverse reaction to RCM was so intense that the provost (a strong supporter of RCM) was moved to rename the effort *value-centered management* to defuse the charge that the initiative ignored many if not most of the broader functions of the university. Coincident with the name change, the administration introduced a series of criteria to govern supplementary appropriations to units from state funding. These included "special efforts to improve teaching," "interdisciplinary cooperation," "improvement in student quality," and efforts to reach out to the public.

This conversion did not work, however, because as a practical matter business models do not lend themselves to a broadening of mission. They remain dependent on one-dimensioned metrics—partly because they are financial systems but also because a metric such as credit-hour generation is easily quantified while most other objectives are not. Whereas using credit hours to define even a highly sophisticated numerical tuition-attribution scheme is relatively easy, it is difficult to develop quantitative measures for other performance criteria. RCM systems quickly deteriorate into one concrete numerical performance index and a series of imperfectly defined ideals, thus reaffirming the belief that an academic unit receives incremental tuition from *any* incremental credit hours, with no countervailing quantifiable presumptions in favor of any of the other goals. In some cases, budgeting systems have been supplemented by special arrangements that look a great deal like incremental budgeting.

Interdependence

All financing systems are vulnerable to manipulation, and RCM is no exception. The problem is that the various units of any complex organization are irretrievably interdependent—in their uses of physical plant and administrative support, in their shared responsibilities for instruction, and in their joint research missions. In this regard, the difficulties with the RCM model should not have been a surprise to anyone. The notion that efficiency within large organizations might be improved via internal financing mechanisms that simulate competitive markets has a decades-long history. In 1955, Paul Cook published an article in the *Journal of Business* that suggested that subunits of large organizations might be managed as semiautonomous businesses.[8] Relationships between these divisions would be quantified by systems of transfer prices that were intended to simulate sales in open markets. Outsourcing was advocated (although that term was not used), and a number of other authors suggested that if an open-market supplier quoted prices to one division that were lower than those charged by another division internal to the umbrella firm, then those lower prices should be accepted on the grounds that the company's own subunit had failed a market test.

Cook's analysis produced an important insight—that the principles of transfer pricing could be applied only in situations in which the operational interdependence between units was limited to only one or two aspects of production. Indeed, much of the work was intended to demonstrate how one would construct a series of cross-unit taxes and subsidies that would take account of and compensate for those few interdependencies.

Because the internal pricing idea could not be carried out without corresponding analyses of interdependence and the design of compensating taxes, it was rarely implemented, even on a trial basis. In business, the interdependence between subunits in large organizations proved to be much greater than what was permitted by the prerequisites of the model.

Applications of RCM to research universities face the same problem. The interdependencies are far-reaching. Students who enroll in one unit take courses in another, research programs cross both school and disciplinary boundaries, facilities acquired and maintained by one unit are shared by another, central administrative services (such as admissions, housing, financial management, and library services) are used in different degrees by different units, and so on. To the extent that any business model fails to take account of these interdependencies, it amounts to a blank check in a bottom-line environment. Faculty can be urged to manipulate their membership in joint-research ventures to funnel more overhead and central support to their own units, teaching units can increase their offering of inexpensive lecture courses, schools and colleges can launch new revenue-generating programs regardless of their quality or merit, interdisciplinary teaching programs can be forced into endless negotiations over the appropriate distribution of the credit-hour revenues, and so on.

We observed efforts to tinker with the formulas to deal with such dysfunctional behavior. For example, a formula that credits 100 percent of the tuition (or even 75 percent) to the enrolling college provides an incentive for the enrolling college to admit more students who take many of their credit hours in another college. Decreasing that credit to 50 percent for the enrolling college and 50 percent for the credit-generating college might stem some of that behavior or might not. Or crediting 100 percent of the distributed indirect cost recovery to the college that sponsors a grant proposal stimulates pressure on faculty appointed in multiple units (or faculty engaged in research proposals with colleagues in another unit) to put their proposals through one unit rather than another. Research grants from foundations that do *not* bring full overhead may be unwelcome by schools and colleges that have to pay taxes on expenditures to their central administration. This can discourage faculty efforts to seek funding from nongovernmental sources, even when there are good reasons for doing so.

Complexity of Overhead

Finally, determining appropriate costs has proved to be difficult. In every university, the central administration provides services that are used by all of its units. It provides financial services, plant and maintenance services, security services, administrative services, and library and computer services. Should these costs be attributed to the units as though they were direct expenses? If they are not, then a unit that expands revenues from operations that incur costs across the entire institution (including the central administration) will profit unduly from an underestimation of total cost. If they are, then someone has to engage in the complex accounting task of attributing all central costs to individual units, an expensive and contentious undertaking. Complex cost-attribution formulas are not usually a high priority for universities, and they would ultimately be converted into rules of thumb that are as arbitrary as a system that entirely ignores cost attribution.

7

Faculty Unionization: The Limits of an Industrial Model

Collective bargaining in higher education is relatively common in certain sectors, especially among full-time faculty in two-year colleges. It is more common in the public sector than the private sector and in certain sections of the country that have traditionally been sympathetic to union movements—the West Coast, the industrial Midwest, and New Jersey and north on the East Coast. The union movement has extended to graduate students as well: the first two graduate student unions were recognized at the University of Wisconsin (1969) and the University of Michigan (1970). In contrast, tenure-track faculty members at the nation's elite research universities are not unionized and are unlikely to become so. Among the ten research universities in our study, none has a unionized tenured faculty, and only two have unions representing non-tenure-track faculty.[1] Graduate student unions are more common, at least among publicly supported universities: all five public institutions in our study have graduate student teaching assistant unions, although one has a very small membership.

Many faculty and staff in the universities in our study see union membership as incompatible with the intellectual independence and the spirit of communal inquiry that is traditional to these institutions. In spite of this, national union movements are expanding among both graduate student teaching assistants and non-tenure-track faculty. At a time when unions across the country are losing membership, organizing drives among NTT faculty are becoming more common. In this chapter, we explore why and with what effects.

Yeshiva

Any discussion of the unionization of faculty in higher education in the private sector must reckon with the highly influential 1980 United States Supreme Court decision in the case of *National Labor Relations Board v. Yeshiva University*. In that case, the Court ruled five to four that the professors at Yeshiva University had enough influence over university governance to be considered managers. As managers, they were not eligible to bargain under the National Labor Relations Act.

This decision has severely limited the opportunities for tenure-track faculty to organize successfully on private campuses and has even encouraged some universities to challenge existing unions—sometimes successfully.[2] The main issue for existing unions and for new unionization drives has been the extent to which faculty have managerial authority within their individual institutions. However, it is not clear how "managerial authority" is to be measured. In the highly publicized case of a unionization drive at the Sage Colleges, the National Labor Relations Board (NLRB) reviewed the participation and voting records of faculty on several university committees and concluded that faculty do have managerial roles.[3] In a few other schools, the NLRB has conducted similar reviews and come to the opposite conclusion, allowing union drives to continue. In the end, the decisions have all been matters of judgment. The process has not produced any simple quantitative index of degree of managerial control, and even if someone did try to create such an index, it would be vulnerable to challenge.[4]

Although these issues have arisen again and again in higher education across the country, they are invisible in the elite research institutions in our study. Tenure-track faculty members in research universities have considerable influence when they choose to exercise it, and they know it. Even if the NLRB had concluded that a unionization drive could be allowed under the Supreme Court's decision in *Yeshiva*, such a drive would be unlikely to succeed (or even be initiated) at elite universities.[5]

The same is emphatically *not* true for non-tenure-track faculty, especially those who work full time. Even though they occasionally serve on university committees (particularly curriculum committees), their roles are better described as informed advisors than as full participants in final decisions. Given no legal barriers to their organizing, we expect that more non-tenure-track unions will form, even within our university set, unless university leaders address issues of concern.[6]

Although NTT faculty unions are not yet widespread in the universities in our study, our experience with a recently formed union at the University of Michigan, the Lecturer Employees' Organization (LEO), led us to ask university administrators on all of our campuses their thoughts about unionization. Some non-tenure-track faculty members see unionization as an attractive option, and we were interested to learn whether administrators have thought seriously about that possibility. In general, unionization did not rank high among administrative concerns. Most of our interviews with university administrators revealed little understanding of the reasons driving unionization in academic settings.

What Drives Non-Tenure-Track Organizing?

The geographical distribution of unions in higher education suggests strongly that the broader political climate is one important determinant of successful drives to establish academic unions. Some states have yet to pass enabling legislation or only recently did so. We focus on two factors that contribute to the expansion in union activity among NTT faculty—the loss of homogeneity in the teaching forces in higher education and the lack of managerial experience of academics who deal with substantial populations of non-tenure-track faculty.

Loss of Homogeneity

In the past, most graduate students, especially in the humanities and social sciences, saw themselves as apprentices to the regular professoriate. They were psychologically aligned with the tenure-stream faculty even if they had not yet joined their ranks. Full-time non-tenure-track faculty members were mostly in time-limited positions that, for them, could also be viewed as stepping stones to eventual membership in the regular professoriate.

Times have changed for both graduate students and non-tenure-track faculty. Not only do graduate students in the humanities take longer today to finish their PhDs, but they lack confidence about their futures as professors.[7] The number of tenure-track positions in the humanities is not equal to the number of recently minted PhDs who seek them. It is not unusual today to hear a teaching assistant in English or history worry that this might be his or her "last regular teaching job."

Non-tenure-track faculty members also know that the market for their services in tenure-track positions is tight. They realize that their non-tenured status may become permanent. Thus, members of what was once a relatively homogeneous teaching force who expected to attain (eventually) full membership in the professoriate can no longer be confident of that result. A situation that once might have been described only as a temporary apprenticeship has become for many a permanent condition or a way station toward nonacademic employment.

The burdens of apprenticeship are sustainable only if they ultimately lead to regular membership in a craft. If apprenticeship status in academia becomes permanent, the identification of graduate students and NTT faculty with tenure-stream faculty breaks down. In practice, tenured faculty are often appalled by the vehemence and vituperation expressed by non-tenure-track colleagues and students during organizing drives and in negotiating settings. They correctly recognize a breakdown in the sense of academic community that is a part of their own heritage, but they do not always recognize that the academic community itself has lost the homogeneity that forestalled such behavior in the past.

This breakdown extends to the relationship between tenured faculty and administration. Traditionally, top administrators (presidents, provosts, and deans) came from the ranks of the faculty—often from faculty in the same institution or a peer university. This practice preserved a cultural uniformity across the institution and weakened the "us versus them" attitudes that come naturally to individuals embedded in hierarchical relationships. However, the division between instructors and administrators has been exacerbated by a growing emphasis on commercial business practices in higher-education management and a growing practice of recruiting academic administrators from unfamiliar university systems or even from outside the academy. What was once organizationally a kind of genteel hierarchy has lost its gentility—at the cost of an increased sense of estrangement even between tenure-track faculty members and university administrators.[8]

Lack of Supervising and Negotiating Experience

Non-tenure-track faculty (and graduate students) are hired and super-vised by faculty and department chairs whose own goals and incentives do not necessarily include human-relations skills. Department chairs do their jobs on a rotating basis, with little supervisory training, experience, or even interest.

As a general rule, department chairs in research universities have two top priorities: they seek to preserve their research careers while they take on (often unwanted) administrative responsibilities, and they also need to recruit and retain outstanding new faculty into their departments. In fact, department chairs are usually chosen by their peers because they are believed to excel in exactly these two areas. They are highly respected by their colleagues because of their research prominence, and their col-leagues believe that this same prominence will prove to be effective in recruiting the "best" new faculty.

It is not easy for anyone unfamiliar or inexperienced with a research university environment to appreciate the extent to which these two objectives eclipse ordinary managerial responsibilities—such as treating supervisees with consideration and respect. Some academics do not deal effectively or even decently with lower-status employees, and this creates circumstances ripe for missteps that can mushroom and create serious personnel problems that provide grist for the organizing mill. In this light, any institution of higher education with a faculty or graduate student union probably deserves one.

One often reads of the plight of part-time NTT faculty who are not given proper support facilities—such as office space (or at least desk space in an office), computing facilities, or access to employee benefits. These deficiencies are actually *not* typical of the research universities in our study. Part-time and full-time NTT faculty are given spaces to meet with students, have access to computers, and most are eligible for bene-fits.[9] At the same time, they are often denied the inexpensive benefits of respect and personal status. At one institution, they are not even called *faculty*. At another, NTT faculty members were not permitted to eat in the faculty dining room. NTT faculty members sometimes are not included on department lists. For example, a lecturer (not from one of our schools) related that she had been given a "great teacher" award by her institution but missed the awards ceremony because she did not know about it. She was not invited, apparently because lecturers were not included on departmental distribution lists.

Most department chairs are not inhumane or contemptuous of NTT faculty (although some may be), but they are not selected or rewarded for their human-relations skills, and it does not occur to them to develop these skills. They are driven (and *driven* is the appropriate term) by concerns that push aside the niceties of interpersonal relations, and they sometimes end up treating non-tenure-track faculty members without respect. One may tell a part-time lecturer two weeks before the start of a term that he or she will be rehired to teach his or her usual course. This can happen even though there was no real uncertainty about hiring but rather because notification simply took a back seat to other concerns.

Within academia, collective-bargaining drives and negotiations after a union is in place can be bitter and unproductive. One reason for this is that few participants on either side have much negotiating experience. Few administrators in our study had any experience with a union, and given the turnover of students and some NTT faculty, the leaders of even long-standing unions are frequently novices in their roles. In many cases, neither side is experienced or accomplished in the business of creating mutual understanding, of developing sympathy, or of proposing compromise.

Related to their inexperience with collective bargaining is the tendency of administrators, faculty, and graduate students to be influenced by extravagant newspaper images of industrial conflicts of the early and mid-twentieth century. The language of conflict (*struggle, fight, strike,* and so on) arises throughout the rhetoric of organizing drives, and this campus rhetoric is often more strident, thoughtless, and uncompromising than is found in today's industrial settings, which benefit from experienced leaders and long-standing relationships. The public utterances of faculty union leaders often mimic the rhetoric of the industrial labor movement—partly because many are politically liberal with long-standing sympathies with the union movement and partly because their understanding of industrial relations is often limited to representations found in the media, which highlight conflict rather than the mundane features of routine negotiation.

Academic labor organizations have little in common with those in industry. Nevertheless, the outward appearance of industrial conflict is reinforced by the fact that organizing activities are often sponsored by unions that have industrial histories and have not been associated with education in the past. For example, the United Automobile Workers (UAW) is a prominent sponsor of academic unions. In other cases, organizing drives have been sponsored by organizations such as the American Federation of Teachers (AFT) and the National Education Association (NEA), which have traditionally concentrated on K–12 schools and not higher education.

A prominent exception is the American Association of University Professors (AAUP), which is an academic organization with a long history of support for tenured faculty. AAUP was founded at a time when the tenure track was the norm among faculty, and it has protected the institution of tenure, supported the general economic interests of faculty, and ensured that faculty play an active role in the management and policy directions of their institutions (that is, in recruiting new faculty, in searching for new administrators, and in governing the processes of promotion and tenure). In 1972 the AAUP reversed an earlier course and stopped opposing faculty bargaining. The AAUP has now become a player in the academic union movement, with seventy collective-bargaining chapters, some of which are organized in conjunction with the AFT.[10]

The heritage of industrial unionism has a second unfortunate aspect for universities, which is the creation of unrealistic expectations on the part of both sides of the relationship. Academic administrators fear the consequences of faculty organization far more than circumstances warrant, while union members expect financial gains that are unlikely to be realized. The economic circumstances of industrial organizations of the mid-twentieth century bear no resemblance to the economic circumstances of academic organizations today. The midcentury corporations that controlled automobile manufacturing, steel making, and transportation enjoyed enormous market power. There were many fewer competitors in their markets, and they faced no significant threats from abroad. The term *monopoly* would overstate the case, but corporate concentration was sufficient to generate substantial financial surpluses, and organized labor sought to share in those surpluses. Thus the focus of the industrial union movement was on "splitting a large and growing economic pie" through negotiations that increased wages, expanded benefits, and created generous retirement programs at the expense of profits and shareholder returns.

Academic institutions (for reasons set out in detail in chapter 4) are engaged in an intense competition with one another, and the costs of that competition pose a constant threat to their financial viability. As in other highly competitive environments, there is no large, expanding pie to divide. As a result, faculty unions do not appreciably affect economic benefits. After providing data that reveal no significant impact of union membership on faculty compensation, Ehrenberg, Klaff, Kezsbom, and Nagowski comment: "With little bargaining power and very few monopoly rents to extract, one should expect unions to have a very small impact on faculty salaries."[11] In any case, there is an easy market test for this conclusion. The undisputed economic gains received by industrial unions in the mid-twentieth century created a significant increase in demand for employment positions in unionized plants compared to others. This was a reaction to their superior levels of compensation. There does not appear to be any comparable phenomenon in higher education. We see no evidence that employment in a unionized faculty is preferred to employment anywhere else.

Moreover, a number of states do not allow public-sector unions to strike, which denies them powerful collective action. Not surprisingly, negotiated outcomes for faculty on campus are different from those in industrial settlements. While new NTT faculty unions sometimes make modest catch-up gains in salary, most negotiated changes have focused on status and community membership in the form of improved personal recognition, longer contract terms, earlier notification of contract renewals, improved prospects for promotion, and enhanced status.[12]

The historical association of academic bargaining with industrial unionism is gradually giving way to a recognition that tight financial circumstances limit the economic gains that are available from collective bargaining on campus. Instead, the academic union movement is turning away from discussions centered on traditional issues of division and turning toward common resource concerns. An April 2007 conference at Hunter College, hosted by the National Center for the Study of Collective Bargaining in Higher Education and the Professions, avoided a focus on the potential of unionization to improve economic returns to members, examining instead the "Struggle for Resources: A Joint Management/Labor Challenge." This new direction reflects the recognition by university and union leaders that the division of resources cannot be a primary focus because the resource base itself is so limited. In the case of public universities, the old model of internal conflict is gradually being replaced by jointly sponsored diatribes on funding shortfalls—particularly the unwillingness of state and federal agencies to provide levels of financial support that are comparable to what existed in the past.

Attributes of Non-Tenure-Track Faculty Union Settlements

Given the economic circumstances of higher education, we would expect universities to acquiesce to union demands only if they require modest expenditures. Given the management deficiencies described above, we would expect that much could be done to improve the sense of well-being of non-tenure-track faculty at a modest cost. Many of these new practices could have been implemented before a union came along to demand them.

Status

An almost universal complaint voiced by non-tenure-track faculty is their low status on campus. This is often a reflection of administrative practices that offer no significant recognition to NTT faculty—such as inclusion on department membership lists and representation at faculty meetings. Not surprisingly, status issues rank high among the concerns expressed in union organization drives. (This is in contrast to industrial negotiations, in which status does not appear as an issue at all.)

The effectiveness of union organization in dealing with status issues is not clear. Some issues (such as thoughtless administrative neglect of non-tenure-track faculty or the relatively minor economic costs of instructional support) can be addressed in contract negotiations. The more subtle issues (such as the unpleasant and demeaning attitudes that are sometimes displayed by internationally known, research-oriented, tenure-track faculty) are harder. Indeed, organizing drives might worsen the atmosphere rather than improve it by emphasizing the separation between unionized NTT faculty and nonunionized tenured faculty.

Status issues may account for the fact that union organization is still relatively unusual in our ten research-centered universities. If membership in a union signals that one is not really among the elect, unionization might not be a popular option. Prestige comes from any association with these particular institutions. "I am on the faculty at X University" (without mentioning NTT status) is heard often enough to suggest that the prestige (and the fear of its loss) outweighs many other inconveniences that are attendant on actual positions.

Status, or the lack of it, is built into the culture of a campus, and it is embedded in the attitudes of many tenure-track faculty members toward their non-tenure-track colleagues. In this dimension of culture, our ten universities vary considerably. In some cases, non-tenure-track faculty are recognized as essential contributors to the instructional enterprise, are welcomed into department meetings, and are accorded respect as contributing members of the faculty. In other cases, non-tenure-track faculty are nearly invisible to the tenure-track faculty and may not be acknowledged to be faculty at all.

Job Security

All NTT faculty union agreements place job security at or near the top of their priority lists, and lack of job security is one defining characteristic of non-tenure-track faculty. In industrial settings, union contract clauses provide job security through systems of seniority that span entire plants or even entire corporations. Similar clauses are found in some higher-education contracts as well (often described as "bumping rights"), but these are much more limited in scope. One cannot bump a teacher of

French literature into a position teaching mathematics, and hence teaching contracts in higher education always include a clause that ensures that no faculty member will be moved into teaching in a discipline in which he or she is not qualified. The fact that higher education is composed of such a wide variety of specialized disciplinary skills places an intrinsic limit on the extent to which a contract in higher education can provide the level of job security that traditional seniority clauses offer in industrial settings.

Nevertheless, there are significant opportunities for improving security. One of our universities sent letters of reappointment to all one-year lecturers. Four months later, the school sent the lecturers a letter warning that a deficit in the state budget might prevent it from rehiring them, creating enormous insecurity. In the end, that university did rehire those lecturers. A decade ago, almost all the universities in our study were offering one-year or even one-term employment contracts with no formal assurances of renewal. A non-tenure-track instructor might be told officially of reappointment only a few weeks before a term was to begin, despite the fact that he or she had been reappointed annually for years to teach the same courses. Unwillingness to make long-term commitments to experienced NTT instructors is demoralizing and, as a practical matter, is usually unnecessary.[13] Faculty contracts are increasingly creating multiple-year appointments for more experienced non-tenure-track faculty, thereby creating a kind of security that does not conflict with the essential operations of the institution. The same changes are occurring in nonunion settings as well, reflecting an acknowledgment that the cost of making these accommodations is not high.

Today, all of the universities in our study offer health and life insurance to non-tenure-track faculty members who are appointed at an 80 percent fraction or higher over an academic year. Most require only 50 percent. In the past, if that individual was not reappointed for the following year, the coverage would stop at the end of the term, leaving insurance over the summer to be replaced from the individual's own resources. In many cases, that summer gap was not covered by the university even after a new appointment was offered the next year. This circumstance is eliminated by multiyear appointments. Even in the case of the one-year appointments offered to those without significant seniority, most research universities have devised mechanisms to provide health coverage across the intervening summer. These costs are relatively modest, but they mean a great deal to NTT faculty members.[14]

Finally, most observers recognize that a job-security clause in a contract is not equivalent to tenure as it is traditionally understood—even if the term *tenure* appears explicitly in the contract. We have noted that a faculty member with traditional tenure has access to an extremely time-consuming and cumbersome appeal and grievance process. It can take years to operate, and at least one step requires faculty review. If the faculty do not support the termination, it can happen only in the most egregious cases of individual malfeasance. The job security that is offered by a union contract (even if it uses the word *tenure*) is substantially weaker. Faculty employment contracts include termination procedures in fairly precise detail, and these usually have time lines that are much shorter than those associated with traditional tenure procedures.

Whether unionized or nonunionized, NTT faculty members on the campuses in our study generally *do* have access to the faculty grievance process and the protections to academic freedom that arise from faculty culture. When they unionize, they rely on contract provisions rather than the regular faculty process, and this may or may not be seen as an improvement.

Job Actions

The final difference has to do with the effectiveness of the most potent weapon of traditional industrial unions—a massive withholding of service. State law in many states prohibits public employees from striking. Where strikes are permitted, there have been some well-publicized efforts in higher education by graduate student teaching assistants, by unionized faculties at Wayne State University, Eastern Michigan University, and so on. We have not seen strikes as yet among NTT faculty at our two elite institutions with faculty unions, although the unions are relatively new.

Beyond state law, another significant barrier to job actions in higher education is the personal commitment that individual instructors have both to their disciplines and to their students. They have chosen teaching careers because they want to convey what they understand about their fields to students. Effective teachers establish strong rapport with their students and accept a personal obligation to help them pursue rewarding and successful lives. A strike or almost any sort of job action flies in the face of the sense of mission that drew faculty into their professions in the first place. Through their classroom interactions, faculty members develop personal allegiances to their students, and such allegiances often transcend even their own personal interests. It is not unusual for instructors to demonstrate solidarity with striking colleagues by rescheduling their classes off campus, thus maintaining their commitments to their students while avoiding the appearance of not supporting the job action. In this sense, the position of faculty in an academic union is different from the position of an industrial employee whose relationship to customers is entirely anonymous and even impersonal.[15]

Put most baldly, the underlying philosophy behind an industrial strike is to demonstrate to management that the cost of granting wage and salary benefits is less than the cost of being shut down. The strike presents a simple financial tradeoff to management: lose money by paying better, or lose money by not operating. Union members face a similar tradeoff: lose money by not being paid, or lose money by accepting a lower wage. Industrial collective-bargaining settlements represent the convergence of these two tradeoff decisions.

The peculiar nonprofit structure of most higher-education institutions does not create a comparable set of choices. College administrations have no obligation to report profits or dividends to shareholders, and thus there is no practical way to make them the economic targets of a strike. They share with faculty a strong sense of commitment to students (as well as to the health of their institution), they deplore and are distressed by any action that is seen to harm either one, but the simple economic tradeoff that typically confronts a profit-making corporation is absent. About the best that an academic union can hope for is that academic administrators will be embarrassed and perhaps humiliated by the pickets, signs, marchers, emails, blogs, and articles in student newspapers—but even these come at the high cost of threatening even further the sense of community and common purpose on which any educational institution depends.

Professionalizing the Non-Tenure-Track Faculty Role on Research Campuses

As some prestigious research institutions have come to understand and appreciate the educational contributions of NTT faculty, they are responding with improved status, greater job security, better benefits, and higher salaries. We find that these improvements are as likely to occur in nonunionized as in unionized environments. The tendency of campuswide employment agreements to specify uniform levels of compensation may work to the disadvantage of some NTT faculty. We did hear from some who felt that unionization limited their merit increases and introduced undesirable inflexibility in their job arrangements.

Three examples from our study illustrate these improvements for NTT faculty, and none occurred on a campus with a unionized workforce. Duke University initiated its *professor of practice* (POP) appointment system in the late 1980s to end a system of rolling one-year appointments that offered little security and low pay. Duke limits its POP population to 20 percent of the faculty in arts and sciences. An assistant professor of practice initially receives a three-year contract. Faculty members receive promotion increases as they move up the promotion ladder to associate or full professor of practice, and their contract terms may increase to five, seven, or even ten years. Full-time POPs have full benefits at Duke and may vote and serve on the academic council. They compete for "dean's leaves," which serve the same professional development function as sabbaticals. Appointments to the POP system fill faculty slots; therefore, departments debate the desirability of this type of appointment and the tradeoff implicit in choosing a POP rather than another tenure-track hire.

Northwestern University uses a promotion system for lecturers in arts and sciences, first to senior lecturer and then to college lecturer. Many are on three- or five-year contracts. In the Kellogg School of Engineering, NTT faculty members have "rolling" contracts that extend for five years from the current date of employment, directly addressing issues of notice and job security.

Washington University lecturers start with one-year contracts and eventually move to three-year agreements. After five years of employment, lecturers may become senior lecturers and become eligible for a tuition benefit for their children. Although none of these universities has solved all of the issues of concern to non-tenure-track faculty on their campuses, all have moved to improve conditions of employment in various ways, even in the absence of organizing drives. We see these trends as constructive and believe more university leaders should learn about them and consider appropriate responses for their own campuses. We return to this issue in chapter 9.

8

Do Hiring Practices Matter?

We began our study of faculty hiring practices on research-oriented campuses because we believed that hiring practices have led to substantial changes in the overall composition of the teaching staff at those schools. These changes have not gone unnoticed. The expansion in the numbers of instructors who are not on the tenure track is widely condemned even though there is very little solid evidence that it warrants condemnation. It turns out that asking questions about the effects of these changes has proven to be much easier than answering them. Does increasing the number of non-tenure-track faculty lead to lower-quality undergraduate teaching and impede student learning? Does it portend the end of the tenure system and weaken the authority of faculty to speak their minds in and out of the classroom? What are the long-term implications for graduate programs when so many academic jobs go to individuals who are willing to work without tenure? What are the implications for the centrality of research in a system where faculty governance increasingly empowers non-tenure-track faculty whose interests may be limited to their own roles in the classroom? What does the increasing specialization of academic roles in research *or* teaching—rather than research *and* teaching—mean for a desirable balance in the mission of universities? In this chapter, we look at the information that we do have on how the changing faculty workforce has affected the quality of undergraduate education, graduate education, university governance, academic freedom, and the future of the research university.

Undergraduate Education

Some faculty members at research universities are passionate about the importance of research to undergraduate education. They support this position by providing examples of popular and enthusiastic instructors who have been research inactive for years and who teach ideas that lost their currency decades ago. Others believe with equal passion that heavy emphasis on research, especially at elite research universities, detracts from undergraduate teaching.[1] Supporters of this position point to the brilliant researchers who confront undergraduates with intellectual sophistication that is beyond their capacity and who do so in a dry, impersonal manner that loses their students' attention entirely. Our own administrative experience provided many examples of both scenarios. The predominant view in the institutions in our study is that involvement in research makes faculty *more* effective as educators.[2] Proponents of this view argue that faculty members who are active in original research convey current and relevant material to their students and also instill a spirit of open-mindedness, critical thinking, and intellectual excitement that are more important than simple facts and formulas.

Given how passionately these views are held and how central the issue is for higher education, one might expect to find credible, systematic studies that settle the argument once and for all. Despite repeated calls for assessments that compare the educational effectiveness of different colleges and universities, however, we cannot deliver. We cannot measure the educational value that is added from college entry to graduation (and beyond) in a way that permits meaningful comparisons across universities and across types of instructors within universities.

Several national efforts seek to measure whether universities are delivering on their promises and purposes. The National Survey on Student Engagement (NSSE) measures whether college seniors *believe* that they have made educational gains in college and whether they would go to the same institution again, knowing what they do about their experiences there.[3] The Collegiate Results Instrument (CRI) asks graduates six years after commencement to report about their jobs, skills, abilities, salaries, and any formal study after their baccalaureate degrees.[4] Whether the measures reflect subjective judgments or objective achievements, authors acknowledge that they cannot claim their results to be valid indicators of the effects of the college attended or of the different types of instructors.

Others have looked at national data to see if differences exist in student achievement (such as graduation rates or performance on graduate or professional school admissions tests) across institutions typed by institutional emphasis on research or teaching or both.[5] Because the differences in learning observed across institutions could be attributed to many other things (such as the types of students enrolled or the student-to-faculty ratio), these studies try to control for such differences to develop conclusions about college effectiveness. Ehrenberg and Zhang find that graduation rates decline when public universities hire large numbers of NTT faculty.[6] Alexander W. Astin's 1993 book, *What Matters in College? Four Critical Years Revisited*, reports that instructors with a strong "teaching orientation" are more effective than those with a weaker teaching orientation in inspiring student learning as measured by most observable student outcomes. Astin also reports that the "teaching orientation" and "research orientation" of a faculty are negatively related. On the other hand, the "research orientation" of the faculty at an institution has a *positive* effect on student LSAT scores.[7] When Astin looks at the faculty within a single university, he finds a "weak *positive* relationship between research productivity and teaching effectiveness."[8] He concludes that "there is no inherent contradiction in a faculty member's being both research-oriented and effective in teaching." Astin expresses the view that the problem resides in *institutional* policies: "Most institutions that hire large numbers of Research-Oriented Faculty apparently give little priority to effective undergraduate teaching."[9] This conclusion suggests that the type of faculty member hired is less important than the climate created within a university for high-quality undergraduate instruction.

Comparing the effectiveness of education delivered by tenure-track (research-active) faculty and non-tenure-track faculty within a single institution is difficult, although we have noted that opinions are strongly held and forcefully offered.[10] There are suggestions that student learning is increased when student and faculty contact outside of the classroom is increased and that students spend more time with full-time than with part-time faculty.[11] This approach does not settle the matter for universities with full-time NTT instructors who spend their careers devoted to the education of their students, inside and outside of the classroom.

The practice of evaluating courses or academic programs is surprisingly undeveloped, even in our most distinguished universities. The only evaluation that is routinely applied in the classroom is that of student grades. However, student grades, while reflecting levels of performance, do not in themselves measure *change* in what students know or how they think—and achieving that change is the point of instruction. Worse, while grades are generally accepted as indicators of student performance, they are rarely seen as potential indicators of instructional performance. When student performances in two sections of a large multisection course are different, the grades are often adjusted to standardize grade distributions rather than examined as possible indications of differences in teaching effectiveness. This practice may stem from an unwillingness to disparage the teaching effectiveness of a colleague, but it ignores the real issue of teaching effectiveness.

Not only are universities unable to demonstrate what students learn from attending expensive classes for four years, but they invest heavily in educational innovations without determining their effectiveness. Institutions that prize advances in knowledge based on systematic inquiry rarely evaluate academic programs in similarly rigorous ways.[12] Although systematic evaluation is possible, occurs occasionally, and is not prohibitively expensive, we found no careful assessment of the comparative teaching effectiveness of faculty members by type of appointment in any of our ten universities. Nor did we find any comparisons reported in published sources. The information that does exist does not address the central question: do students learn more, less, or about as much from NTT faculty (who are less likely to be at the cutting edge in research) than from TT instructors at elite research universities (where tenure is awarded based largely on a positive evaluation of scholarship)? We suspect that the answer would vary according to the subject matter being taught, especially whether the course focuses on a field of study in rapid transition or one, such as calculus or elementary language, that does not change much from year to year.

The usual time to evaluate a faculty member's contributions to education is when renewal, promotion, or tenure is considered. For formal evaluations of teaching, faculty use a variety of tools, including peer visits to classes, examination of syllabi and assignments, teaching statements, and student assessments of courses and instructors. None of these measures is outcome-oriented, and the only one that uses standard measures and permits affordable comparisons across faculty and courses is the student assessment (or "course evaluation"), which is itself often dismissed by faculty as merely a measure of popularity and not an indicator of learning. Indeed, we are aware of no empirical demonstration of a positive correlation between evaluation scores and any objective measure of student learning.[13]

However crude student evaluations may be, we did not find better measures in use on any of our ten campuses. One of our disappointments was to learn that the quality of teaching evaluation is no better (and in some cases is worse) at the nation's most prestigious research universities than elsewhere. In 2006, the Harvard faculty was still debating the idea of requiring student evaluations of undergraduate courses.[14] Most (but not all) of our ten research universities do require student evaluations of courses, but some of these do not have standard questions that permit comparisons across departments, schools, and colleges. Even where student evaluations are routine, we know of no university that regularly compares student teaching evaluations of instructors by type of instructor.

Familiarity with the data systems at our own university did enable us to combine datasets in a way that produced some tentative comparisons, but no other institution had assembled comparable data. From our limited sample, we found suggestions that student evaluations were, on average, highest for non-tenure-track faculty, followed by tenure-track and tenured faculty, followed by graduate student teaching assistants. The data provided in table 8.1 are drawn from the following question asked of students in all courses in arts and sciences at Michigan over twenty-three terms of teaching: "Overall the instructor was an excellent teacher." Responses are provided on a scale of 1 (lowest) to 5 (highest), and the data in the table are averages of these scores over the twenty-three terms of teaching.

Table 8.1
Student evaluations of instructors by type of instructor, controlling for course level and department, in arts and sciences, 1989–90 to 2000–01 (Q: "Overall, the instructor was an excellent teacher")

	Tenure-track faculty	Non-tenure-track faculty	Teaching assistant
Lower-division scores:			
Chemistry	3.63	4.06	4.02
Economics	3.82	4.41	3.88
English	4.30	4.63	4.17
Philosophy	4.08	*	4.05
Physics	4.13	4.31	3.82
Psychology	4.46	*	4.03
Upper-division scores:			
Chemistry	3.88	4.09	4.05
Economics	4.04	4.64	4.00
English	4.46	4.76	4.09
Philosophy	4.27	*	4.03
Physics	4.14	*	*
Psychology	4.41	4.65	4.18

*Insufficient cases to permit meaningful analysis.

To make reasonable comparisons, we must disaggregate the data by department and level (such as, first two years, second two years, and graduate courses) for two reasons. First, evaluations are systematically higher for upper-level courses. Upper-division (junior and senior) courses are rated more highly than lower-division courses, and graduate courses are typically evaluated at the very top. Because tenure-track faculty members do most of the graduate teaching, and lower-division courses employ most of the NTT faculty and graduate students, an average across all course levels would incorrectly suggest that TT faculty members are evaluated much more positively than NTT.

Second, course evaluations vary systematically across disciplines. Those in English are consistently higher than those in economics, for all types of instructors. Because English departments employ far more NTT faculty than do economics departments, the disciplinary differences (if not controlled) would inappropriately elevate the overall evaluation averages for NTT.[15]

As table 8.1 shows, NTT instructors usually (but not always) obtain higher scores than other types of instructors. On the one hand, this is not surprising since non-tenure-track faculty members are hired as teachers and are evaluated with teaching performance in mind. In contrast, tenure-track and tenured faculty members are evaluated using a complex set of factors that include teaching but emphasize scholarship and peer review. On the other hand, this outcome may be surprising given how much has been made of the positive impact of faculty research orientation on student learning and the less adequate academic training of NTT as compared with TT faculty.[16] Graduate student teaching assistants are evaluated at the very bottom in the humanities. They are beginners, and they face many demands beyond their teaching responsibilities.[17] The picture is more mixed in other fields, where TAs sometimes score higher than TT faculty. The best of the TAs do well in the classroom, especially with experience, training, and mentoring. Some of our universities offer new teaching assistants well-developed programs of training; others do not.

Ratings in student course evaluations are usually quite compressed. If the questionnaire asks for responses on a scale of 1 (lowest) to 5 (highest), the responses are almost always limited to 3, 4, and 5 with a mean of 4 or higher. This pattern does not leave much room for distinctions among instructors. Nevertheless, because the student opinions that are summarized in course evaluations are frequently the only pieces of evidence of teaching performance that can be compared across faculty members, they often assume unreasonable importance in hiring, retention, and promotion decisions. Given the compression that is characteristic of student scores, sometimes great importance is attached to even small differences. At the universities in our study, teaching performance may be a weak second consideration in the standard performance mantra for TT faculty (research, teaching, and service), but even so, fear of poor evaluations can affect educational decisions by those faculty who feel most vulnerable (such as assistant professors and NTT instructors), especially those, who are evaluated almost solely on evidence of their teaching success. We talked with a well-respected, long-term NTT educator at one of our institutions who wanted to experiment with her teaching method but decided the risks were too great because of possible negative student reactions. She was not confident enough of her security and status to take a chance on receiving poor student evaluations.

Prior research suggests that *expected* grades are strongly correlated with student evaluations, and it is possible that more vulnerable instructors give higher grades than do tenured faculty.[18] None of our campuses adjusts student evaluations for grade distributions on any routine basis, although we did observe two social science departments that did.

Student opinions do not capture whether the course material is current, and a central argument for the superiority of research faculty in the classroom is that they keep up with the latest scholarship in their fields and, in fact, contribute to it.[19] Assessing this aspect of education requires expert evaluations of syllabi, lecture material, assignments, and so forth, or it requires tracking student success in subsequent graduate study in the field. These sorts of measures are not available.

One of the strongest arguments in support of having research-active faculty in the classroom is that they are able to engage students in research. The growth of undergraduate research programs over the past twenty years has added a significant strength to undergraduate educational experiences, especially at research universities.[20] Today, about 85 percent of students at the Massachusetts Institute of Technology participate in at least one experience in the Undergraduate Research Opportunities Program (UROP) during their college years. Other universities have followed MIT's lead, and all of our ten universities now have active undergraduate research programs. The National Conference on Undergraduate Research, established in 1987 with a few hundred participants, now attracts thousands of student presenters from more and more research institutions.

Involving undergraduates in research activity across the university is a special strength that research universities bring to the undergraduate experience. Highly ranked professional schools, including law and medicine, offer extraordinary opportunities to undergraduates to learn as apprentices from leading scholars across an array of fields, much broader than what is available at liberal arts colleges, community colleges, or comprehensive universities. At all of our research institutions, undergraduates work with faculty and graduate students in the laboratory and experience the excitement of original discovery firsthand. This type of activity is rarely evaluated in any systematic way, although participation as mentors for undergraduates has become a part of the promotion files of tenure-track and tenured faculty. Undergraduate research programs are such a common feature of higher education today that they have their own professional association.[21]

Another growth area in higher education is off-campus study and experiences. Universities have added to the traditional junior year abroad a wide variety of programs, including combined internship and study experiences in the nation's capital and study and experiential learning overseas. Undergraduates at all of our ten institutions have a set of opportunities to advance their cultural understanding and develop strong work skills.[22]

UROP and off-campus experiences are usually developed by tenured faculty who take advantage of their international connections and established research programs to involve undergraduates. After the programs are established, they may be taken over by non-tenure-track faculty, but they gain academic respectability in part via the stature of the tenure-track faculty who are involved in their founding, and they maintain respectability through TT faculty involvement as leaders, participants, advisers, and evaluators.

NTT faculty appear to satisfy students with the specific courses that they teach. The available data do not allow an evaluation of whether part of that satisfaction might be due to easier grading practices. At Michigan, students taught by NTT faculty report more positive assessments of their in-class experiences and more positive views of the accessibility of their instructors. NTT faculty members are popular, and many are talented educators. Again, data are not available to evaluate whether the course content offered by NTT faculty always remains at the cutting edge of understanding, but neither are we able to evaluate whether TT faculty continue to update their courses throughout their careers. None of our schools employed a strategy of hiring NTT faculty only for those kinds of courses that are least likely to require constant updating. Instead, they are asked to teach the introductory survey courses in fields such as biology, psychology, and anthropology, where knowledge advances quickly.

Universities seem to hire more and more NTT faculty to teach undergraduates without having any convincing evidence that this is in the best interests of students. Whether the increasing use of NTT faculty in lower-division teaching strengthens or weakens an undergraduate curriculum remains for us an open question. We do agree that effective programs that offer undergraduate research and off-campus experience require tenure-track participation, but the administration and organization of these programs may actually be most effectively provided by NTT faculty. The powerful learning experiences that can come from involvement in research projects or academic experiences off campus are rarely evaluated in a systematic way.

Graduate Education

Tenure-track faculty members at research universities are heavily invested in graduate education. By training graduate students, they stay current in their fields, teach their specialties, benefit from talented research assistants, and populate universities around the world, thereby spreading and enhancing their own reputations. These same faculty members strive to have their graduate students placed in postdoctoral and faculty positions at leading universities and in leading research laboratories. This desire often translates into a fairly narrow view of success. Indeed, PhD students often avoid talking with their advisers about their interests in teaching-oriented jobs or nonacademic employment for fear of losing the respect of their mentors, who might regard a NTT academic position as a sign of placement failure.

Most tenure-track faculty at elite research universities expect to teach at least one graduate course every year, and some teach only graduate courses. This drive to train graduate students contributes to increases in numbers of NTT faculty who fill otherwise unmet needs in undergraduate teaching and advising. By turning over more and more undergraduate education responsibility to NTT faculty, however, the TT faculty may be placing their own focus on research and graduate education at risk in the long run. Legislators and parents expect undergraduates to benefit from exposure to the distinguished faculty they support through tuition and state allocations. When tenure-track faculty members teach few undergraduate classes, the political consequences can threaten the existence of graduate programs and weaken arguments for additional funding. In the mid-1990s, the then-president of the University of Rochester, Thomas Jackson, proposed eliminating four graduate programs as part of a larger plan to refocus the institution around undergraduate education. The most controversial of the four was the graduate program in the department of mathematics, which was targeted in part because of a dismal reputation for undergraduate teaching. The decision was eventually reversed after the department agreed to revamp the curriculum and commit more resources to undergraduate instruction. The mathematics community subsequently sponsored a conference focused on improving undergraduate education.[23]

We have already addressed the question of why many students undertake graduate training when their career outcomes may be NTT appointments. The other side of this same question concerns the willingness of graduate programs to turn out large numbers of PhDs, even in areas without robust job markets. The answer appears to be the strong interest on the part of the faculty to have graduate students to populate their own classes and to participate in their research programs. Especially in subjects such as chemistry and engineering, large graduate cohorts are needed to support laboratory research, and most graduate students are supported on research grants. In the humanities, social sciences, and mathematics, research grants large enough to support graduate students are less common. Financial support packages typically depend on a combination of fellowship dollars and teaching assistantships.

Graduate student teaching assistantships and NTT faculty positions compete directly in some cases. When faculty can support graduate students on research assistantships, fellowships, or government training grants, they do so and leave extra undergraduate teaching to NTT faculty. When these other forms of graduate support are unavailable, TT faculty almost always prefer hiring graduate students to NTT faculty on any type of continuing basis.[24]

Faculty members are not insensitive to the possibility that they are producing more PhDs than the tenure-track market can absorb. A view is commonly expressed (especially in the humanities and some social sciences) that the total number of graduate students should be limited so that each graduate can be placed in an appropriate academic job after degree completion. This is another area, however, in which competition among universities leads to suboptimal outcomes. A conclusion that the total numbers of PhDs should be reduced provides no guidance as to which programs should be cut back. Especially in the strongest departments, faculty believe that enrollments should be restrained *elsewhere*—a view that is not shared by lower-ranked institutions. Top departments may maintain their graduate numbers, with the natural consequence that many new PhD recipients can find only NTT positions.

Unlike undergraduate admissions, which are managed centrally, graduate admissions are highly decentralized. Decisions are made in departments and sometimes in subgroups within departments, with the predictable result that there are no effective administrative constraints on numbers. At one of our universities, graduate student numbers increased by 50 percent over three decades while undergraduate and faculty numbers remained roughly constant. University leaders were delighted at the growth of research dollars that made this expansion possible, and claimed (with no evidence) that undergraduates received the same high-quality educational experience regardless of the size of the graduate student body.

Graduate schools are rarely major players relative to the other schools and colleges within elite universities. In fact, not all universities have a graduate school. When they do exist, they are assigned responsibility for overall graduate student numbers and quality, even if they lack effective mechanisms for control. Graduate schools sometimes award enough of the graduate fellowship dollars to influence admissions decisions at the graduate level in those fields that require university support.[25] They sometimes pass rules that require tuition payments from graduate students every year between admission and completion, a practice that discourages students from lingering without progress. In at least one instance, the provost set rules on central subsidies for research assistantships that influenced the number of graduate students who could be supported on grants. However, these approaches are all indirect. Departmental faculty members at elite universities jealously guard their influence over graduate admissions numbers and decisions.

As union-negotiated contracts make TAs more and more expensive at public universities (by covering tuition, stipends, health care, and so forth), instruction by graduate students can become much more expensive than instruction by NTT faculty. In our interviews, we sought insight into whether these higher costs might have influenced graduate student admissions. On the one hand, we have already expressed our skepticism toward a proposition that cost comparisons might lead to conscious decisions to replace one instructional type by another. On the other hand, a policy that transmits the full costs of teaching assistants down to the department level is bound to have budgetary consequences. A department may have no choice but to hire more NTT faculty if it is not given the resources to support the number of graduate students it would like.

How this affects decisions about graduate admissions depends on whether departments rely heavily on TA positions for graduate student financial support and whether departments are responsible for all of the TA costs. Universities that place budgetary responsibility at the department level may some day find that departments have moved toward more NTT faculty and fewer graduate student instructors to maintain the department's ability to hire TT faculty and pay good salaries—although we have no evidence that this has happened to date. One of our public universities handled all tuition waivers for TAs centrally (at the provost level) so that tuition costs would *not* become a factor in department decisions about who should teach. Another passed tuition costs down to the college level and made deans conscious of the full cost of hiring TAs rather than NTT faculty. This cost consciousness extended even to the cost differential between in-state and out-of-state TAs as well as between liberal arts and professional school TAs. This university had the largest number of NTT faculty and the highest ratio of non-tenure-track to tenure-track faculty in our study.

Shared Governance and the Locus of Decision Making

In chapter 3, we outlined the challenges and complexities of leadership and administration in higher education. In that chapter, however, we did not address the question of how the faculty as a whole participates in formal policymaking or how that participation may be altered by the introduction of large numbers of NTT teaching or research faculty.

The phrase most often heard in describing faculty involvement in decision making is "shared governance"—a concept that suggests that administrators make policy decisions only after serious consultation with the faculty, which tends to consider issues in a format reminiscent of a New England town meeting. Anyone outside of academia might regard such a structure (and culture) as utterly unworkable, and in most settings it would be.

There are two institutional factors that have made shared governance possible. The first is a general understanding that the issues over which the parties have authority are partitioned, with faculty having primary responsibility for curriculum, faculty selection, graduate student admissions, and similar academic matters, while the administration has primary responsibility for nonacademic matters such as budget, fund raising, construction and maintenance, security, and residential facilities. The actual areas of overlap are usually limited to such areas as undergraduate admissions, library acquisitions, laboratory equipment, and technical support. This partition of responsibility reduces the overlap of influence and ensures that the unwieldy structure suggested by a generic term such as *shared governance* is less of a problem than it might at first appear.

The second factor is that both faculty members and administrators traditionally have come from similar (faculty) backgrounds and share a strong set of common values. Faculty members and administrators do not agree on every issue, but they share a general sense of the mission of the university, the relative roles of research and teaching, and even the responsibilities that go with tenure. That shared set of values usually facilitates a shared process and policy decisions that are acceptable to both faculty and administrators.

Faculty members tend to see themselves as independent professionals rather than as part of an organizational hierarchy. If they call a dean, provost, or president their "boss," both parties understand the joke. Presidents and provosts emphasize the centrality of the faculty and regularly refer with nostalgia to their lives as faculty members. We commonly hear presidents say that the best job on campus is the tenured professorship—whether they believe it or not.

While administrators are under pressure from trustees, the legislature (for publics), donors, and the public to demonstrate their ability to achieve concrete objectives, faculty members expect real influence over matters that affect their work life. Moreover, their style of discussion and decision making can require extensive debate and compromise before they can establish a "faculty position" on an issue. College administrations have final authority given the statutory or even constitutional responsibilities assigned to boards of trustees and by them to administrators, but the *de facto* clout of a distinguished faculty can be powerful. Examples abound of administrative proposals that are significantly revised or even reversed after faculty dissent. In this regard, distinguished research universities are different from other higher-education institutions. Distinguished faculty members can leave if their views are not accommodated, the threat of departure carries real influence, and serious differences between administration and faculty are sometimes resolved by forced changes in university leadership.

An environment of shared values is critical for shared governance to work. That is why faculty members often express suspicion or even hostility toward top administrative appointees who come from outside academia or from universities of lesser rank. They fear a breakdown in the paradigm of shared values, without which the model of shared governance becomes unworkable. A president who chooses to implement his or her *de jure* authority without accommodating the faculty's *de facto* authority risks undermining the entire governance structure of the institution.

A similar threat to governance accompanies the infusion of large numbers of non-tenure-stream faculty because they also introduce a different set of values. Tenure ensures that decisions (even those that a faculty member opposes openly) will not threaten his or her employment. The same is not true for NTT faculty. The introduction of specialists who do not hold tenure has brought with it values and fears that are sometimes quite different from those that formed the foundation of existing governance systems. In particular, specialists introduce new types of self-interested economic factors that can substantially change the course of a department, college, or even an entire university.

When tenured faculty and senior administrators ignore the growth in numbers of specialists (both in teaching and in research) on campus, they do not pay adequate attention to the implications of this growth for university mission and direction. When NTT faculty numbers balloon and NTT faculty have voting rights, resource allocations and curricular decisions may change. One arts and sciences college proposed changing the foreign-language requirement for undergraduates in ways that would encourage the study of low-enrollment languages. This proposal had the full support of the dean and much of the tenured faculty. According to college bylaws, however, such a change required a vote of the college faculty, and NTT faculty had full voting rights. Attendance was low at all but the most controversial college faculty meetings, but in this case, NTT faculty in the most heavily enrolled language areas, fearful of losing their positions, turned out in large enough numbers to vote the proposal down. Another university decided to grant voting rights to research faculty in department, college, and university bodies, including hiring and promotion decisions. Unlike the NTT faculty, who show up for faculty meetings, the research faculty usually do not. This expansion of voting rights created quorum problems that rendered two science departments unmanageable, and chairs could not gather enough voting members to make hiring decisions. A third example arose in a department that hired NTT faculty in such numbers that they eventually outnumbered the TT faculty and controlled many departmental decisions, especially around the undergraduate curriculum. An external review was highly critical of that curriculum. The department was put in "receivership," was reorganized by the dean's office, and most of the NTT faculty were dismissed.

With full voting rights comes the possibility that untenured specialists will sway votes on issues that are judged likely to affect their own conditions of employment. Research faculty who rely on "soft" grant funds become ardent advocates for policies that provide university funding during temporary lapses in grant support. They also demand professorial titles that permit them to be principal investigators on grant proposals. Teaching faculty who rely on enrollments to justify their continued employment monitor proposed changes in graduation requirements that might affect enrollments in their own fields. As NTT faculty numbers have grown, tensions have sometimes developed over the emphasis on research and graduate education, and as research scientists have gained professorial status, voting rights have shifted attention in hiring and promotion away from educational contributions toward funded research volume.

The long-term threat imposed by this dispersion in interests (between faculty and administration and within the faculty itself) is that faculty governance will become more contentious and difficult. To our minds, the only plausible replacement would be increased centralization—a change that might well imperil the dynamic and shared environment that has made American higher education so effective.

The involvement of NTT in faculty governance varies considerably across and within our ten research universities. Some NTT faculty are not part of the "regular" faculty and have no voting rights on academic matters, other NTT faculty have voting rights limited to curricular matters, and still other NTT faculty have full voting rights at the college or university levels (even if not in departments). Some universities limit voting rights to full-time NTT faculty, while others require a certain fraction of an appointment (80 or 50 percent). Some require a certain number of years of continuing appointment. A number of universities have given professorial titles to research faculty and, in some instances, given them full voting rights.

Consistent with the tradition of decentralized decision making in large research universities, different rules of governance are developed in different units and at different levels. Departments decide on their own bylaws, except in areas of promotion and tenure where the college and university establish standards and operating procedures. To be welcoming, some departments (especially in the humanities and social sciences) grant broad voting rights to NTT faculty in curriculum and graduation requirements, while others (especially in the sciences and engineering) generally restrict voting rights on such matters to TT faculty. In some cases, NTT faculty members have voting rights in a department but not at the college level; in other cases, we find just the reverse. Access to voting rights tends to be correlated with other aspects of NTT appointments. In a few cases, NTT faculty are still limited to specific terms of service with no possibility of renewal. This constraint usually goes hand in hand with limited governance rights and restricted NTT involvement in decision making. In other settings, NTT faculty spend their entire careers at the same university and are often active in faculty governance;

they show up for faculty meetings, even when many TT faculty do not.

Presidents and provosts pay little attention to the rules of faculty governance except when it frustrates their initiatives. Because they are largely unaware of the numbers and growth of NTT faculty members at their own institutions, academic leaders rarely confront the implications of a changing academic workforce for faculty governance at any level.

Academic Freedom and the Future of the Research University

Over time, more and more of our nation's faculty workforce is hired explicitly without tenure. What difference does this make to academic freedom? This is another area in which the volume of opinion dwarfs the volume of systematic evidence.

The *Chronicle of Higher Education* reports regularly on controversies arising from academic writing or classroom discussions, including criticisms of Israel or Palestine, interpretations of evolution, gay and lesbian studies, nudity or sexism or ethnic stereotyping in art, and archaeological evidence in biblical studies. The academic values most prevalent in American universities today protect free expression in education and research. Faculty members might dislike what a colleague says or writes, but few would support administrative action to fire or discipline that colleague for unpopular views. Presidents, provosts, and deans share that perspective. The faculty grievance procedure requires a step of faculty review, and that step often discourages punishment in the first place.

We believe that the same value system extends to non-tenure-track faculty in the universities in our study, but it is not necessarily as effective in those cases. The difference lies in greater maneuvering room for an administrator who wants to take action against a NTT employee. There is a strong presumption against firing a tenured member of the faculty except for cause (such as moral turpitude) at an elite university. If the academic unit in which the faculty member works is discontinued, tenured faculty who stay are usually reassigned to other academic units. Alternative duties, often not demanding, may be assigned to permit flexibility in the face of illness or family concerns. Periods of research inactivity are tolerated as long as there once was work of high quality or there is the promise of high-quality work to come. Even deadwood status is addressed by smaller than average (or zero) salary increases but not termination. In light of this, the grounds for dismissing a tenured member of the faculty are narrow and require a compelling case.

The presumption of continuing employment for NTT faculty is not nearly as strong as it is for tenured faculty. It relies on a continued need for service and continuing positive performance. If the unit is discontinued, the teaching need disappears, or the teaching evaluations suffer, dismissal or nonrenewal is likely. That leaves open a wider set of possibilities for administrators to take action that may be a reaction to unpopular ideas but that can be justified as something else. NTT faculty members know this and feel more constrained in their behavior as academics. In practice, the broad license extended to tenure-track faculty under the heading of "academic freedom" applies to NTT faculty but not in equal measure.[26]

Challenges to academic freedom occur every day but not often on the campuses in our study. Based on our own experiences as faculty members and as deans of arts and sciences, we believe that this value system (embodied in tenure) provides important protections for faculty research and writing, especially in the humanities, social sciences, and biology. It also protects faculty who pursue fundamental research with no obvious near-term payoff, scholarship that challenges social norms and widespread scholarly beliefs, projects that span decades, and risky innovations in research and teaching.[27] Although we can identify individual tenured professors who neglect their responsibilities or settle for "barely adequate" rather "outstanding" performance and still benefit from the protections of tenure, we nevertheless believe that the institutionalized value system that protects intellectual expression is critical to the strength of higher education in the United States. This is the perspective on tenure that has motivated the written positions of the AAUP for decades, and it is a perspective that repeatedly comes to the fore in discussions of non-tenure-track employment.

9

From Dilemmas to Action

"Begin at the beginning," the King said gravely, "and go on till you come to the end: then stop."
—Lewis Carroll, *Alice's Adventures in Wonderland*

We started with a deceptively simple question: are the nation's most elite research universities hiring non-tenure-track faculty to teach undergraduates? Having learned that the answer is yes, we then asked three additional questions: how and why are they doing this, and what are the consequences of these hiring practices for higher education? To answer these questions requires understanding how and why things happen the way that they do in research universities. Accepted wisdom—that the numbers of non-tenure-track faculty have increased because university leaders decided to hire cheap, temporary labor to save money—is an oversimplification of reality that misidentifies decision makers, assigns nonexistent motives to those decision makers, and suggests changes in policy that will not produce desired results. NTT faculty members can be tremendous assets for a research university if they are hired for the right reasons and if they are constructively integrated into the university community. The problem is that most universities hire NTT faculty without regard to any overall staffing strategy, they fail to evaluate their contributions adequately, and they often treat them simultaneously as second-class citizens and as full voting members of the faculty.

We have identified six dilemmas facing university leaders today. The choices they make to address these dilemmas will shape the composition of the teaching faculty and the future of higher education in this country.

Dilemma 1: Whether to Invest in Management Information Systems

Most CEOs have a good estimate of the number of employees at their firms and feel reasonably confident in the employee numbers that are provided by their human resources offices. This is not so for university presidents. Most can easily cite the number of tenured and tenure-track faculty or positions at their institution, but few have any idea of the number of non-tenure-track faculty members who are teaching their students. Moreover, it is difficult and in some cases impossible for them to find out. The data and management systems at many of our most prestigious institutions are inadequate to the task. Even if the systems exist, the data come from departments and programs at different times and offer uncertain accuracy. Yet every year these same institutions respond to questions from their boards as well as from federal and state governments about these very numbers, and their answers imply a level of precision that does not exist.[1]

While it might seem obvious to an outsider that universities need to improve management information systems immediately, this is a dilemma for university presidents and provosts. Many do not see this as a serious need. We suspect that many university leaders have no idea just how inadequate their current systems are and how much error exists in what these systems produce. They rarely appreciate the policy consequences that follow when the numbers that they produce are taken literally by the public, the media, and a legislature. Occasionally, a crisis intervenes to force improvements. There is nothing quite like a successful union organizing drive to focus attention on the need to develop accurate non-tenure-track numbers. In such cases, adjustments are usually piecemeal, however, and rarely lead to comprehensive improvements of management information systems.

Even if presidents recognize the need for new systems, developing them is a daunting task. University leaders can successfully pursue only a limited number of major initiatives during their terms of office. Converting to a campuswide (or systemwide) information system can be disruptive and controversial, and it can frustrate the staff members who have to develop and use it. In the absence of university systems, each department and college has developed its own operating system and habits over decades, and they are apparently working well; chairs and deans resist making changes merely to meet data needs of higher-level management. Indeed, they do not welcome higher-level interference and prefer to hold their information at a local level. Large investments in systems that provide little obvious benefit for academics on the ground can quickly be labeled wrong-headed, wasteful, and intrusive.

Moreover, the cost can be high. Information system redesigns for a large campus can easily cost $50 million (or even $100 million) over several years. This is equivalent to the endowments for dozens of full-time tenure-track faculty positions or the renovations of dozens of laboratories. Investing in such an expensive system requires foresight and determination from the top. Strong leadership is needed to dedicate scarce resources to information systems that faculty do not value even as enterprising faculty members clamor for more research support, graduate student support, and facility upgrades. Moreover, the payoff from improved information will come years in the future when benefits will not likely accrue to those currently leading the institution. An improved data system is hardly the type of achievement that will bring lasting fame to a university president.

Dilemma 2: Whether to Review Campus Governance

Every major university practices some form of shared governance in which faculty members play pivotal roles in hiring, recommending promotions and tenure, establishing curricula, applying for research dollars, publishing scholarship, and so forth. The success and reputation of the university depends on these processes. Traditionally, tenured faculty members constitute the regular faculty and oversee the details of academic governance. Because in the past the numbers of non-tenure-track faculty were small, few administrators paid much attention to NTT voting rights or to governance issues in general.

The number of non-tenure-track faculty has grown dramatically over the past three decades, however, including a mushrooming growth in the numbers of research specialists. These specialists in teaching and in research have become essential to their institutions, but their interests and priorities are often different from those of traditional faculty. Teaching specialists may not place a high value on research, while active research faculty frequently describe the end of a class (or the beginning of a summer break) as an "opportunity to get back to work." University leaders who ignore the impact of these narrower perspectives on campus governance do so at their peril.

At the same time, presidents of large, distinguished research universities focus more and more on external relations (such as fundraising, government relations, and international presence) to the neglect of internal affairs (such as the academic enterprise on campus). If presidents become involved with individual faculty recruitment or retention, their attention is inevitably drawn to the research stars. They do not have the time, length of tenure, or inclination to get to know members of the non-tenure-track faculty. Relatively few of the tenured faculty become familiar with non-tenure-track faculty either. They typically pay little attention to NTT hiring, renewals, or evaluations, even though these "invisible" colleagues can and do affect decisions and outcomes on important academic questions.

Cultural differences from one college to another or from one department to another can produce different governance practices. Those that are inclusive can find themselves in situations where the NTT faculty who show up for critical votes outnumber the TT faculty, thereby skewing the results in ways that divert practice from overall university goals. Those that are exclusive can make valuable NTT faculty feel marginalized and promote disgruntled employees and eventual union success.

We know of no instance in which a president or provost spent time becoming familiar with the various governance practices on campus before some emergency had arisen. Governance, like management systems, can seem mundane and unimportant given the press of other business. Yet a scan of the governance practices on campus can provide university leaders with useful information before they try to bring about meaningful academic change. In some cases, they may decide that it is desirable to establish certain campuswide standards for faculty governance.

Dilemma 3: Whether to Compete

University presidents compete for academic rankings (whether or not they are meaningful), athletic rankings, hospital rankings, students and student test scores, distinguished faculty and faculty prizes, research dollars, state support, size of library holdings, size of fundraising campaigns, memberships in exclusive organizations, return on investments, bond ratings, presidential salaries, mentions in the press, and much more. Rather than improving efficiency, heightened competition stimulates spending wars, complicates efforts to cooperate and work across boundaries, and permits distinguished faculty to earn more for teaching less. Presidents compete because they believe, whether valid or not, that rankings affect student applications and choices, private donations, faculty recruitment and retention, approval of board members, government and corporate support, and their own salaries, opportunities, and prestige. They worry that their universities' standings and their own reputations will slip if they opt out of the competition. Yet competition in one domain costs money that might be spent on other priorities. Clearly, deciding how (and when) to respond to heightened competition in one or more domains can present a dilemma for university leaders.

Some leaders do decide not to compete in certain arenas. Seven of our schools compete in Division IA football and three do not. For years, Northwestern University played in the Big Ten football conference but did not invest precious university resources in a huge stadium and did not recruit players with questionable academic records. With a change in presidents, the university began competing more aggressively. For years, Ohio State University invested more in football than the University of Michigan did, with luxury boxes in the OSU stadium and state-of-the-art athletic training facilities on the Columbus campus. In recent years, despite considerable opposition from faculty, some alumni, and several regents, Michigan leaders decided to compete more aggressively by establishing luxury boxes, seat taxes, and lavish facilities.[2] Other alumni were pressing Michigan to compete with OSU. University leaders must decide about their priorities and the appropriate directions of the university.

Another competitive arena is attracting and retaining faculty stars. Most presidents, provosts, and deans believe that faculty members should interact with students—even if they win Nobel Prizes or MacArthur Awards. A few limit the number of terms that a faculty member can be on leave and absent from teaching duties, even if the person is performing public service at the highest levels. Some decide they will not compete in certain professional areas (such as medical or dental schools) so that the schools will not divert financial resources from the liberal arts and change the overall character and priorities of the professoriate on campus. Others bow to faculty requests for long leaves of absence and special, reduced teaching responsibilities in an effort to please star faculty.

Establishing expectations for senior faculty—that they will teach undergraduates and introductory courses from time to time, that teaching is a central part of their faculty role (along with scholarship), that their instructional contributions will be meaningfully evaluated as part of salary and promotion processes—is the job of university leaders. It requires backbone every day in the face of one individual after another asking for apparently meritorious exceptions. Occasionally, a faculty star may decide to leave for another university that makes fewer demands, and the loss can be painful even as it sends an important signal about campus values. If any university leaders can alter the conditions of competition for star faculty in ways that might affect higher education more broadly, they are the leaders of the most prestigious and wealthy universities in this country, such as those that are the focus of this study.

Dilemma 4: Whether to Emphasize Investment Returns to Education

University leaders are constantly honing arguments that emphasize financial returns to education—for the individual who graduates from college, for the state economy (or region) in which the college is located, and for the nation as a whole. Presidents make these arguments even though they leave little room for the important roles of universities in inspiring creativity in the arts and humanities, preserving heritage, or understanding history and culture. Leaders do so to convince state and federal legislators to budget more for higher education, to convince parents that paying high tuition is worth it, and to convince donors to give more generously to their alma maters.

Deciding to emphasize financial returns is not so much a dilemma as an apparent necessity. What may present a dilemma is how seriously to balance economic arguments with others that emphasize the value of studying and doing scholarly work in the humanities, arts, and social sciences. Some university leaders continue to highlight the importance of areas of work and study that do not translate immediately into economic gains. Without sustained support, vital academic domains of arts, humanities, and social sciences will suffer. As new cohorts of students and their parents become focused on acquiring job skills in college, undergraduate enrollments shift from the humanities to engineering and business. In some cases, universities have sent powerful signals about the importance of the arts and humanities at the same time that they make their return on investment arguments. For example, the president of MIT dedicated a $100 million discretionary gift to the School of Humanities, Arts and Social Sciences; Michigan has an endowment of more than $45 million for the Institute for the Humanities.

Dilemma 5: Whether to Borrow Business Models from the Private Sector

Some presidents and provosts were eager to adopt responsibility-centered management as a budget reform to encourage greater unit-level attention to priorities and especially to focus more attention on efficiency. Others saw the results of RCM at peer universities and decided not to adopt the system at their own.

RCM and its relatives are aimed both at increasing revenues at the unit level and at controlling costs. The incentive structures created by these systems often have unintended consequences, such as encouraging departments or colleges to offer courses or programs primarily to generate revenue (new undergraduate majors, applied masters programs, or writing or math or language courses), even if those courses or programs do not attract serious faculty attention or achieve real distinction. Such offerings can undermine other programs within the same university by drawing away enrollments. They can also scatter university resources by multiplying offerings in a particular intellectual domain across several colleges on the same campus. RCM in particular encourages units to hire non-tenure-track faculty to teach courses that are not central to the unit's or the college's mission. If these faculty engage in research, they work on topics far afield from the focus of the hiring unit (such as writing in

[handwritten marginalia: why can't these be economic booms too? (both to individual student consumers and to the state)? AND cast science, engineering as fundamentally tied to liberal education, ethics, citizenship]

an engineering school) and work in a unit that is ill-equipped to assess the quality of their scholarship. Decentralized decision making has great advantages, but without strong and sustained central leadership, it can encourage decisions that are not in the best interests of the university as a whole and not compatible with core academic values.

Much can be gained by using business thinking in revising budgetary processes, without adopting business systems wholesale. For example, a good business model may highlight the importance of allowing units to carry over balances at the end of the year so that they are not encouraged to spend on unnecessary purchases just to move remaining balances from their books. One might also quantify the costs of reduced enrollments, excess space, or wasteful energy usage. Rather than importing a system such as RCM in its entirety, university leaders can engage in conversations with units about these matters and try to adjust allocations in ways that do not create perverse incentives. For those who choose to adopt an RCM-like system, leaders need to understand the possible undesirable consequences and recognize the challenges inherent in attempting to ensure that subunits act in the interests of the university as a whole—in the face of adverse incentives that the administration itself has established.

Dilemma 6: Whether to Professionalize Non-Tenure-Track Positions

Presidents seem either to ignore non-tenure-track faculty members or to try to replace them with teacher-scholars on the tenure track. A third approach would be to decide on the necessary roles on campus that are best filled by NTT faculty and to determine the number of non-tenure-track hires needed to fill those roles, to plan for that number, and to treat the hires as valued members of the academic community. This approach requires deciding what the appropriate circumstances might be and what conditions of employment would attract talent to campus, convey respect and value, and create a community of educators rather than a bifurcated system of haves and have-nots.[3]

An appropriate first step would be to understand the different ways that tenure-track and non-tenure-track instructors are treated in various university units. Many of these distinctions in treatment are unnecessary and costless to eliminate. Others cost money but not very much. We believe that university leaders should attend to the working conditions of all of their employees, including the NTT faculty, and eliminate conditions that are demeaning and unnecessarily harsh.

Why might this be a dilemma for a president or provost? First, hiring NTT faculty members "on the cheap" can save money in the short-run and seem appealing under severe budget stringency. Second, attending to the working conditions of NTT faculty consumes time and energy that otherwise might be spent on more mobile tenured faculty stars. Third, decisions to hire NTT faculty have been essentially delegated to departments, and central involvement can be seen as intrusive. Fourth, improving the working conditions for NTT faculty might be seen by some as an effort to undermine tenure. Nevertheless, based on our study, we conclude that NTT faculty members have become an essential resource for research-intensive campuses and that campus leaders should acknowledge this and create working conditions that will attract and retain talented individuals for those posts. It is in the institution's best interest for NTT faculty to feel that they are valued professional members of the academic community who will be supported in pursuing successful careers.

Dealing seriously in a sustained fashion with each of these dilemmas is not for the faint-hearted, but university presidents and the boards that appoint them will do so if they care about the long-run health of their universities. They might begin by insisting on receiving useful and reliable management information, for without it, informed leadership is impossible. Some universities have well-developed systems, so we know this is possible. The University of Washington and the University of Michigan both invested substantially in information systems some years ago, and they serve as examples of universities that generate valid and reliable answers to many important management questions. University leaders should become familiar with the "shared governance" rules and traditions at the university, college, and department levels before a crisis forces familiarity. The honeymoon period that follows the appointment of a new leader can be a good time to recommend a review of these rules and traditions with an eye toward making changes that emphasize academic freedom and a balance between research and education of undergraduates, graduate students, and professional students that form the core of the university's mission. These are basic building blocks for successful university leadership.

The Triumph of Specialization

This is not the first time in American history that faculty roles have undergone dramatic change. Colleges and universities in this country began as teaching institutions, usually with strong ecclesiastical links. In the eighteenth and early nineteenth centuries, the terms *college* and *seminary* were used almost interchangeably. In the mid-nineteenth century, Johns Hopkins and other institutions in the United States began emulating the great German research universities in which faculty merged teaching with active research careers. A new doctrine of dual faculty responsibilities evolved that rested on the belief that a vigorous and productive research career informs and improves teaching and that effective and committed interaction with students energizes research. This philosophy spread across the United States as faculty and administrators alike emphasized the need for every faculty member to excel in both research and teaching. The research side received an enormous boost after World War II with Vannevar Bush's successful articulation of an important new partnership between universities in the United States and the federal government.[4] The second half of the twentieth century was replete with charges that research responsibilities had come to dominate the teaching function, even though most faculty still believed that each faculty hire should epitomize the ideal balance in the model teacher-scholar.

This balance is in peril today. Tenured faculty members focus increasingly on research as their involvement in undergraduate education declines. Some never see undergraduates. The reason for this is not hard to identify: an increasingly competitive academic marketplace has put a premium on the visibility and prestige of individual faculty members. The market for prominent faculty is intensely competitive, and research visibility plays the most important role in that competition. Elite universities do not compete aggressively for teaching faculty. They compete for faculty whose work will elevate their school's rankings in national research surveys, in government reports on the distribution of research support dollars across universities, in newspaper features, and in the news magazines whose rankings are followed closely by students (and their parents) when they select colleges.

A system that balances research and teaching is gradually being replaced by a system of comparative advantage under which faculty members are being driven to specialize. It may be that everyone would prefer to specialize in research, as that is the more highly compensated of the two activities, but research support is awarded competitively and there is not enough to support everyone. Limited research dollars and careful peer review, limited journal capacity and scrupulous refereeing, and limited capacity of universities to release faculty from teaching coupled with their desire to reserve course releases for their most marketable faculty all contribute to a hierarchy of research support. Because this hierarchy governs both reputation and actual resources committed to research, it becomes self-reinforcing: some faculty come close to doing only research, while others specialize in teaching.

This specialization takes place both within and across colleges and universities. Within universities, it takes the form of increasing disparities in teaching responsibilities and discretionary research support. Active scholars in the humanities at elite research universities expect to teach three or four courses per year; teaching specialists in humanities fields typically offer six or eight. Active researchers in biology average fewer than two courses per year, while teaching specialists in the sciences typically offer four. We also see specialization in service roles. More and more tenure-track faculty resist department service roles, student advising, and even positions of department chair. Some of these—especially the service and advising roles—are assigned to lecturers or professional advisers. Once this happens, it often becomes apparent that the lecturers do a better job than the tenure-track faculty.[5]

Within the broad arena of higher education, specialization of institutions also takes place. Colleges and universities that make no serious claim to be active participants in the national research scene expand. Although almost all research-intensive universities have experienced increases in enrollment, the bulk of the national increase in undergraduate population has been accommodated by schools that focus on teaching. That is, the increased specialization is taking the form of specialized institutions as well as specialized faculty.[6] Indeed, this is the niche that is being dramatically exploited by the for-profit sector. While for-profit institutions probably will not make serious inroads on research-oriented institutions, their rapid growth is evidence that they offer a competitive threat to any institution that focuses only on teaching. They also market the most profitable courses (such as beginning economics, science, or psychology), leaving other universities less able to use financial resources generated from relatively inexpensive courses to subsidize other important but more expensive intellectual areas.

These realignments in employment are ordinary economics, and mirror the standard doctrine that as trade barriers decrease and markets broaden, participants in trading relationships become increasingly specialized. Normally, this type of specialization is considered to be good because it replaces inefficient systems under which each individual carries out a range of activities (whether or not he or she is well suited for them) with a system under which each individual carries out only the activities for which he or she is especially qualified. In this case, however, the change is controversial and even aggressively resisted because it dramatically challenges the philosophy that underlies the self-image of our most outstanding universities—that every faculty member should be a teacher-scholar. This same philosophy leads university administrators, college executive committees, and tenure-review committees to deny tenure to specialists. Persons who "only" teach (lecturers, instructors, adjunct faculty, and so on) and persons who "only" carry out research (research scientists and research investigators) are regarded as ineligible for tenure because their activities do not fit the broader dual-responsibility model.[7]

We would not argue that the dual-responsibility model is wrong but that it no longer captures the full array of faculty roles needed in universities. Once again, our universities are undergoing a significant change in faculty roles. The traditional model conflicts with market-driven specialization that is evident on campuses across the country. University leaders need to recognize these forces and develop plans to manage them if they are to maintain the long-term excellence of our best institutions. Duke University made an early start with its professor of practice system, which acknowledges the university's need for teaching specialists, sets limits on the proportion of faculty entitled to these roles, and establishes procedures for managing these positions (including national searches, professional development opportunities, improved conditions of employment, explicit tradeoffs between hiring professors of practice and tenure-track faculty in each department, scope of participation in university governance, evaluation procedures, and so forth). This specific system is not necessarily the best for all elite research universities, but careful planning around these issues is important for the health of academic climates today and in the future.

Notes

Chapter 1

1. Carnegie Foundation for the Advancement of Teaching, *Reinventing Undergraduate Education: A Blueprint for America's Universities* (Stony Brook: State University of New York, 1998) (also called the Boyer Report); Piper Fogg, "Teaching Your Way to Tenure," *Chronicle of Higher Education*, September 1, 2006, A12; Sara Rimer, "Harvard Task Force Calls for New Focus on Teaching and Not Just Research," *New York Times*, May 10, 2007, A20. Since the Boyer Report was issued, research universities have improved undergraduate education on their campuses significantly. See "Three Years after the Boyer Report," available at http://www.reinventioncenter.miami.edu/BoyerSurvey/index.html#survey01. Despite these improvements, criticisms continue.

2. David Horowitz, *The Professors: The One Hundred One Most Dangerous Academics in America* (Washington, DC: Regnery, 2006).

3. Ernst Benjamin, "Declining Faculty Availability to Students Is the Problem—But Tenure Is Not the Explanation," *American Behavioral Scientist* 41, no. 5 (1998): 716–35; Karen Thompson, "Contingent Faculty and Student Learning: Welcome to the Strativersity," *New Directions for Higher Education* 2003, no. 123 (2003): 41; Carnegie Foundation, *Reinventing Undergraduate Education*.

4. George Borjas, "Foreign-Born Teaching Assistants and the Academic Performance of Undergraduates," *American Economic Review* 90, no. 2 (2000): 355–59; P. D. Umbach, "How Effective Are They? Exploring the Impact of Contingent Faculty on Undergraduate Education," *Review of Higher Education* 30, no. 2 (2007): 91+.

5. Jon C. Strauss and John R. Curry, *Responsibility Center Management: Lessons from Twenty-five Years of Decentralized Management* (Annapolis Junction, MD: National Association of College and University Business Officials, 2002); Lana Low, "Are College Students Satisfied? A National Analysis of Changing Expectations," *New Agenda Series* (Iowa City: Noel-Levitz, Inc., 2000).

6. We do not agree with most of these criticisms because research universities have improved undergraduate education since the late 1980s. Long before the

Boyer Report, at the University of Michigan we initiated a program of first-year seminars that were large enough to accommodate all entering students. These seminars are taught by senior tenured faculty. We expanded undergraduate research opportunities with research-active faculty throughout the university for first- and second-year students, launched theme semesters organized by faculty to add coherence to undergraduate offerings and emphasize interdisciplinary perspectives, and strengthened English-language requirements for graduate teaching assistants. These types of initiatives and more can be seen on all of the campuses in our study.

7. Michael D. Cohen and James G. March, *Leadership and Ambiguity: The American College President* (New York: McGraw-Hill, 1974), 104.

8. For representative scholarship, see the following: Deborah M. Herman and Julie M. Schmid, *Cogs in the Classroom Factory: The Changing Identity of Academic Labor* (Westport, CT: Praeger, 2003); Cary Nelson, *Will Teach for Food: Academic Labor in Crisis* (Minneapolis: University of Minnesota Press, 1997); Cary Nelson and Stephen Watt, *Office Hours: Activism and Change in the Academy* (New York: Routledge, 2004); "Quit Hiring Short-Term, Tenure Track Profs Needed," *Indiana Daily Student*, April 26, 2002, 8; Gary Rhoades, *Managed Professionals: Unionized Faculty and Restructuring Academic Labor*, *SUNY Series, Frontiers in Education* (Albany: State University of New York Press, 1998); Barbara Wolf, Michael Burnham, Andrea Tuttle Kornbluh, and Eliza Combs, *A Simple Matter of Justice*, Disk 2, *Contingent Faculty Organize* (videorecording) (Cincinnati: Barbara Wolf Video Work, 2001).

9. For example, see Roger G. Baldwin and Jay L. Chronister, *Teaching without Tenure: Policies and Practices for a New Era* (Baltimore: Johns Hopkins University Press, 2001); Ernst Benjamin, "Changing Distribution of Faculty by Tenure Status and Gender," Memorandum to the American Association of University Professors Executive Committee, January 29, 1997; Xiangmin Liu and Liang Zhang, "What Determines Employment of Part-Time Faculty in Higher Education Institutions?" CHERI Working Paper No. 105 (Ithaca: Cornell Higher Education Research Institute, 2007).

10. Scott Smallwood, "Disappearing Act: The Invisible Adjunct Shuts Down Her Popular Weblog and Says Goodbye to Academe," *Chronicle of Higher Education*, April 30, 2004, A10–A11.

11. For a summary of these sources of data, see Jack H. Schuster and Martin J. Finkelstein, *The American Faculty: The Restructuring of Academic Work and Careers* (Baltimore: Johns Hopkins University Press, 2006), 96–114. For a focus on medical and professional schools, see Judith M. Gappa, "Off the Tenure Track: Six Models for Full-Time, Nontenurable Appointments," New Pathways Working Paper Series, Inquiry No. 10 (Washington, DC: American Association for Higher Education, 1996). Many of the non-tenure-track faculty at universities are employed in the health sciences and do relatively little undergraduate instruction (Schuster and Finkelstein, *The American Faculty*, 176).

12. For example, we eliminated a practice in one department of hiring lecturers year after year for eight months only, leaving them without health benefits over the summer between appointments.

13. There are many excellent reasons to employ non-tenure-track instructors, who are highly valued members of the university community. Our concerns are that universities have not thought carefully about these reasons, implemented policies that limit hiring for these reasons, or evaluated the results of hiring practices for the quality of education or the health of the academic enterprise.

14. Ehrenberg and Zhang provide evidence of an inverse correlation between the proportion of non-tenure-track instructors and graduation rates across a broad range of universities, but (as in all such studies) the direction of causality is not clear. Ronald G. Ehrenberg and Liang Zhang, "The Changing Nature of Faculty Employment," in Robert Clark and Jennifer Ma, eds., *Recruitment, Retention, and Retirement in Higher Education* (Northhampton, MA: Edward Elgar, 2005), 32–50. We return to this question in chapter 8.

15. John Sexton, "The Role of Faculty in the Common Enterprise University," Report to the Trustees Council of New York University (New York: New York University, 2003). In that speech, Sexton acknowledged that tenured faculty are often disengaged from undergraduates and that teaching specialists play an important role in research universities.

16. See note 8. See also Michael Murphy, "Adjuncts Should Not Just Be Visitors in the Academic Promised Land," *Chronicle of Higher Education*, March 29, 2002, B14; Benjamin Johnson, Patrick Kavanagh, and Kevin Mattson, *Steal This University: The Rise of the Corporate University and the Academic Labor Movement* (New York: Routledge, 2003); Ian Robinson and David Dobbie, "Reorganizing Higher Education in the United States and Canada: The Erosion of Tenure and the Unionization of Contingent Faculty," *Labor Studies Journal* 33, no. 2 (2008): 117–40; Sheila Slaughter and Gary Rhoades, *Academic Capitalism and the New Economy: Markets, State, and Higher Education* (Baltimore: Johns Hopkins University Press, 2004); Marc Bousquet, *"We Are Teachers, Hear Us Roar": Contingent Faculty Author an Activist Culture* (Austin: University of Texas Press, 2006); Marc Bousquet, Tony Scott, and Leo Parascondola, *Tenured Bosses and Disposable Teachers: Writing Instruction in the Managed University* (Carbondale: Southern Illinois University Press, 2004).

17. For example, see American Association of University Professors, "Contingent Appointments and the Academic Profession," in *AAUP Policy Documents and Reports*, 10th ed. (98–114) (Washington, DC: American Association of University Professors, 2006).

18. Eugene L. Anderson, "The New Professoriate: Characteristics, Contributions, and Compensation" (Washington, DC: American Council on Education, Center for Policy Analysis, 2002); Amy L. Caison, "Tenure Trends in Public, Four-Year Colleges and Universities," *Planning for Higher Education* 31, no. 2 (2003): 15–25; Association of American Universities, "Non-Tenure-Track Faculty Report" (Washington, DC: Association of American Universities, 2001).

19. Martin J. Finkelstein and Jack H. Schuster, "Assessing the Silent Revolution: How Changing Demographics Are Reshaping the Academic Profession," *AAHE Bulletin* 54, no. 2 (2001): 3–7.

20. We used a variety of methods in our study. First, we examined a wide range of documents about each of our ten campuses (and other similar campuses), including public information about enrollments, budgets, budgeting processes, faculty size, faculty types, fundraising goals, proposals for reform, levels of support from the state and so forth, over time. These are available on Web sites, in speeches, and in various campus and media reports.

Second, we visited each campus and spent several days in intensive interviews with presidents, provosts, deans, heads of campus data and analysis units, chairs of departments, faculty, faculty union representatives, local higher education experts, and system leaders. In each case, we worked with the president's or provost's office in advance to identify appropriate individuals and set up a schedule. Because we selected campuses where we knew presidents and provosts, we had unusual access.

We asked about the hiring processes for tenure stream and nontenure stream faculty; the budget processes for the campus and the schools and colleges; governance at the campus, school, and department levels; prospects for (or implications of) unionization; and evaluation practices for instruction. We collected reports; data on the numbers of teaching faculty (by type and over time) for the campus as a whole, for arts and sciences, for engineering, and (when available) for specific departments; information on evaluation of instruction as available; and proposals for reform. We explored the meaning of the data we received with our interviewees while on campus and continued these conversations and exchanges by phone and email after our visits, often receiving further data, explanations, and elaborations. In five cases, one of us paid a follow-up visit to meet with campus leaders and/or data experts.

Third, we held discussions with various other experts who have been studying these issues at the American Association of University Professors, the Coalition for the Academic Workforce, the Modern Language Association, the American Association of Universities, and various higher education research organizations.

Finally, we drew on our combined experience of twenty-one years as deans of liberal arts at Michigan, and we read a large number of published books, articles, and reports (higher education organizations, media, government) that bear on these issues.

Chapter 2

1. American Association of University Professors, "1940 Statement of Principles on Academic Freedom and Tenure" (Washington, DC: American Association of University Professors, 1940).

2. The AAUP recommends that after seven years of service, all full-time faculty "should be recognized as having the protections that would accrue with tenure—termination only for adequate cause and with due process." See American Association of University Professors, "Contingent Appointments and the Academic Profession," 104. This practice has rarely been adopted by universities with repect to faculty who are hired into non-tenure-track positions.

3. Other reasons include student preferences and the schedules of varsity athletics. We thank Nancy Weiss Malkiel for pointing this out.

4. Dispersion in compensation levels has been growing in academia, as it has elsewhere in the American economy. Over time, average salaries of non-tenure-track faculty have been falling relative to the salaries of tenure-track faculty. See Ronald G. Ehrenberg and Liang Zhang, "The Changing Nature of Faculty Employment," in Robert Clark and Jennifer Ma, eds., *Recruitment, Retention, and Retirement in Higher Education* (32–50) (Northampton, MA: Edward Elgar, 2005a), 46.

5. Schuster and Finkelstein, *The American Faculty*, 80, 176, 221.

6. The American Association of University Professors (AAUP) issued its first formal report on this problem in 1978, and in its 1986 report, it argued against the growth of non-tenure-track instructors. However, AAUP's presence on elite research university campuses today is weak overall and nonexistent on many. We doubt that many of the tenured faculty on any of our ten campuses are aware of the AAUP's reports on this topic. See "Tales of the Reconstruction: Can Reorganization Save the AAUP?," *Chronicle of Higher Education*, June 27, 2008, A4. In 2006, Schuster and Finkelstein described the growth in full-time NTT faculty as "less visible but hugely significant" (*The American Faculty*, 356). They urged faculty members "to monitor closely the changing distribution of types of appointments" on their campuses. See Jack H. Schuster and Martin J. Finkelstein, "On the Brink: Assessing the Status of the American Faculty," *Thought and Action* (Fall 2006): 60. For the AAUP reports, see American Association of University Professors, "On Full-Time Non-Tenure-Track Appointments," *AAUP Bulletin* 64, no. 3 (1978): 267–73; H. Kasper, F. Bronner, M. W. Gray, B. R. Kreiser, and J. R. Rosenthal, "1986 Report on Full-Time Non-Tenure-Track Appointments," *Academe: Bulletin of the AAUP* 72, no. 4 (1986): A14–A19.

7. See, for example, university faculty headcounts by department in the 1973 version of *American Universities and Colleges* (Washington, DC: American Council on Education, 1973). Also see Finkelstein and Schuster, "Assessing the Silent Revolution."

8. Finkelstein and Schuster describe it as "revolutionary." Finkelstein and Schuster, "Assessing the Silent Revolution," 176. Only 3.4 percent of the full-time faculty in universities in 1969 were tenure-ineligible. Today that number is well over 16 percent.

9. Baldwin and Chronister include research specialists as NTT faculty, whether or not they ever teach, and there has been an explosion in the number of research scientists on the campuses of research universities that is driven by an expansion in externally funded research. Our focus here is on the teaching function, however, and therefore we adopt this narrower definition. Our interviews indicate that the data that are available on the number of research scientists is every bit as difficult to interpret as the data on the number of non-tenure-track instructors. Baldwin and Chronister, *Teaching without Tenure*.

10. Frederic Jacobs, "Using Part-Time Faculty More Effectively," *New Directions for Higher Education*, no. 104 (1998): 9–18.

11. Ernst Benjamin, *Exploring the Role of Contingent Instructional Staff in Undergraduate Learning* (San Francisco: Jossey-Bass, 2003); Bousquet, *"We Are Teachers, Hear Us Roar"*; Gwendolyn Bradley, "Contingent Faculty and the New Academic Labor System: To Defend Academic Values, We Need to Roll Back the Reliance on Contingent Labor," *Academe: Bulletin of the AAUP*, 90, no. 1 (2004): 28; Jane Buck, "Features: The President's Report. Successes, Setbacks, and Contingent Labor: Can Higher Education Thrive When Part-Time Faculty Do Most of the Teaching?," *Academe: Bulletin of the AAUP* 87, no. 5 (2001): 18; Daniel C. Feldman and William H. Turnley, "Contingent Employment in Academic Careers: Relative Deprivation among Adjunct Faculty," *Journal of Vocational Behavior* 64, no. 2 (2004): 284–307; John Hess, "The Entrepreneurial Adjunct: Contingent Faculty Become Commodities in the New Academic Labor Market," *Academe: Bulletin of the AAUP* 90, no. 1 (2004): 37; Monica F. Jacobe, "Contingent Faculty across the Disciplines: News on the Non-Tenure-Track Front," *Academe: Bulletin of the AAUP* 92, no. 6 (2006): 43; E. MacKenna, "Contingent Performances: Between the Acts of Adjunct Faculty," *Journal of the Midwest Modern Language Association* 37, no. 2 (2004): 45–48; James Monks, "The Relative Earnings of Contingent Faculty in Higher Education," *Journal of Labor Research* 28, no. 3 (2007): 487–501; Umbach, "How Effective Are They?"

12. B. Barnetson, "Part-Time and Limited-Term Faculty in Alberta's Colleges," *Canadian Journal of Higher Education* 31, no. 2 (2001): 79; Judith M. Gappa and David W. Leslie, *The Invisible Faculty: Improving the Status of Part-Timers in Higher Education* (San Francisco: Jossey-Bass, 1993); Courtney Leatherman, "Part-Timers Continue to Replace Full-Timers on College Faculties," *Chronicle of Higher Education*, January 28, 2000, A18; Liu and Zhang, "What Determines Employment of Part-Time Faculty in Higher Education Institutions?"; Gary Rhoades, "Reorganizing the Faculty Workforce for Flexibility: Part-Time Professional Labor," *Journal of Higher Education* 67, no. 6 (1996): 626–60; Scott Smallwood, "Faculty Activists across North America Rally for Better Treatment of Part-Timers," *Chronicle of Higher Education*, October 30, 2001, available at http://chronicle.com/daily/2001/10/2001103006n.htm, accessed August 19, 2008.

13. Barnetson, "Part-Time and Limited-Term Faculty in Alberta's Colleges."

14. Piper Fogg, "For These Professors, 'Practice' Is Perfect," *Chronicle of Higher Education*, April 16, 2004, A12.

15. John C. Duncan, "The Indentured Servants of Academia: The Adjunct Faculty Dilemma and Their Limited Legal Remedies," *Indiana Law Journal* 74, no. 2 (1999): 513–86; Robin Wilson, "U. of North Florida to Replace Forty-six Adjunct Faculty Members to Meet Accreditor's Criteria," *Chronicle of Higher Education*, October 30, 2001, available at http://chronicle.com/daily/2001/10/2001103007n.htm, accessed August 19, 2008.

16. We calculate the growth in the use of non-tenure-track faculty for each institution over the period for which we have data and then calculate an average rate of growth for the entire set. There is significant variation around this average. The current ratios of NTT to TT faculty on a full-time equivalent basis fall between .15 for the least reliant college of arts and sciences to over .6 in the most. This compares with national data that show about 60 percent of all faculty are NTT and that about 75 percent of new hires are NTT. Given the differences across institutions, we could not use the ratio in the one university that reported both headcounts and FTEs to standardize the data series by converting headcounts into FTEs or vice versa.

17. Although we did not focus on liberal arts colleges or lower-ranked universities, we know that they also hire NTT faculty, who may do an even higher percentage of the teaching for students in their first two years.

18. These trends have led to the development of pedagogical specialties in the teaching of introductory Spanish, writing, chemistry, and calculus. Specialists write about teaching and learning in their subjects, and some teach introductory courses more effectively than do typical tenured faculty in the field. Introductory language (especially Spanish) is also the area where the lowest percentage of NTT instructors have advanced degrees, where the salaries for instructors are lowest, and where employment practices are often the most problematic.

19. To see disciplinary-specific reports on the growth of NTT faculty, see *Academe Online* at www.aaup.org.

20. Baldwin and Chronister write that the number of full-time non-tenure-track faculty has increased "almost unconsciously, as colleges and universities have made necessary adjustments to shifting enrollment patterns, economic circumstances, and technological advances." Baldwin and Chronister, *Teaching without Tenure: Policies and Practices for a New Era*, 8.

21. "Renowned Engineer Joe C. Campbell Appointed to U. Va. Faculty," *U. Va. News Services*, June 13, 2005, available at http://www.virginia.edu/topnews/releases2005/campbell-june-13-2005.html, accessed August 19, 2008.

22. Laurel Thomas Gnagey, "Provost: Hiring of One Hundred New Faculty Set to Begin," *University of Michigan Record*, January 25, 2008, available at http://www.ur.umich.edu/0708/Jan21_08/04.shtml, accessed September 10, 2008.

Chapter 3

1. Franz Kafka, *The Castle*, trans. Willa and Edwin Muir (New York: Knopf, 1964), 88–89.

2. Cohen and March, *Leadership and Ambiguity: The American College President*, 33.

3. The 2006 taskforce report of the Association of Governing Boards of Universities and Colleges sees this as an important deficiency in university leadership. The report urges boards and presidents to engage more effectively with academic policy and not allow day-to-day emergencies and management to drive out focus on mission. See Association of Governing Boards of Universities and Colleges, "The Leadership Imperative: The Report of the A.G.B. Task Force on the State of the Presidency in American Higher Education" (Washington, DC: 2006).

4. Presidents of universities with hospitals and medical schools have even less time and greater difficulty than others attending to academic matters on campus.

5. American Council on Education, "The American College President" (Washington, DC: American Council on Education, 2007).

6. None had to deal with the incidents of armed campus violence that have occurred at some other universities.

7. Cohen and March, *Leadership and Ambiguity*, 103–04. In the years since Cohen and March wrote, demands on presidents have expanded, making it even more difficult for them to find time for academic matters.

8. Association of Governing Boards of Universities and Colleges, "The Leadership Imperative."

9. Ibid., 38.

10. Art Padilla and Sujit Ghosh, "Turnover at the Top: The Revolving Door of the Academic Presidency," *Presidency* 3, no. 1 (2000): 30–37. Although the American Council on Education published a 2006 study that found that the average tenure increased from 2001 to 2006, the average age of presidents has increased even more, suggesting that turnover will increase in the next decade. See American Council on Education, "The American College President."

11. The one partial exception is John Casteen III, president of the University of Virginia. When hired by Virginia, Casteen was president of the University of Connecticut, but he had previously served as Virginia's state Secretary of Education and, prior to that, dean of admissions and professor of English at the University of Virginia.

12. Goldie Blumenstyk, "Outside Chance for Insiders: Unlike Most Leading Businesses, Colleges Favor External Candidates for Their Top Jobs," *Chronicle of Higher Education*, November 4, 2005, 8.

13. Association of Governing Boards of Universities and Colleges, "The Leadership Imperative," 38.

14. Ibid., 32.

15. An extreme example can be seen in the career of E. Gordon Gee, who is the current president of The Ohio State University and is serving his second time in that position. He previously served as the president of West Virginia University (1981–1985), the University of Colorado (1985–1990), Ohio State University (1990–1997), and Brown University (1998–2000), and as the chancellor of Vanderbilt University (2000–2007). See Ohio State University, *E. Gordon Gee, President: Biography* (Columbus: Ohio State University, 2008), available at http://president.osu.edu/bio.php, accessed January 26, 2008.

16. Association of Governing Boards of Universities and Colleges, *"The Leadership Imperative,"* 33.

17. Ibid., 38–39.

18. The Massachusetts Institute of Technology is the exception. Undergraduate numbers in 2006 were slightly below those ten years earlier at MIT. They dropped after a presidential decision that all first-year students would be required to live on campus. With added dormitory spaces, those numbers will increase. Meanwhile, graduate student numbers at MIT have increased substantially. Universities that require all first-year students to live on campus have a built-in brake on the tendency of admissions offices to overshoot their targets.

19. See, for example, the similar positive responses of admissions directors in institutions as different as University of Rochester (Andrew Brumi, "Freshmen Overload U.R.," *Campus Times*, September 14, 2006, A1+); University of Michigan (Anne VanderMay, " 'U' Overshoots Enrollment Targets Again," *Michigan Daily*, October 27, 2005, A1+); and Macalester College (Brian Martucci, "Unexpectedly High Yield Brings Large Class of '10," *The Mac Weekly*, March 3, 2006, 1).

20. In addition to the unplanned changes discussed here, a number of elite universities (Harvard, MIT, Princeton, Stanford, and Yale) have announced plans to increase the size of their undergraduate student bodies by roughly 10 percent. Some will increase the number of TT faculty on campus, and some will not. Those that do not may find themselves hiring more NTT faculty. See Brian K. Sullivan, "Yale May Expand Enrollment as Levin Sees Ivy League Competition," *Bloomberg News Service*, August 30, 2007, available at http://www.bloomberg .com/apps/news?pid=newsarchive&sid=aH1kNjCfOzVE, accessed August 19, 2008.

21. Among our ten institutions, Michigan, Illinois, Berkeley, and University of Washington all had active graduate student employee unions, the latter three gaining recognition and signing their initial contracts fairly recently. The University of Virginia is in a right-to-work state. It has a graduate student council supported by the annual student registration fee and a small group of students associated with a national union. Graduate teaching assistants at private universities were declared off limits for organizing when the NLRB in 2004 reversed

an earlier decision (see chapter 7 below). At Cornell, graduate students voted down an organizing drive.

22. Paul Brinkman, "Responsibility Center Budgeting: An Approach to Decentralized Management for Institutions of Higher Education," *Planning for Higher Education* 21 (1993): 49–51; William F. Massy, "Measuring Performance: How Colleges and Universities Can Set Meaningful Goals," in William F. Massy and Joel W. Meyerson, eds., *Measuring Institutional Performance in Higher Education* (29–54) (Princeton: Peterson's, 1994); Strauss and Curry, *Responsibility Center Management*; Edward Whalen, *Responsibility Center Budgeting: An Approach to Decentralized Management for Institutions of Higher Education* (Bloomington: Indiana University Press, 1991); Gilbert R. Whitaker, "Value Centered Management: The Michigan Approach to Responsibility Center Management," *The University Record*, January 9, 1995, NA; Gordon Winston, "The Necessary Revolution in Financial Accounting," *Planning for Higher Education* 20, no. 4 (1992): 1–15. Also see various university websites and reports, including those at the University of New Hampshire (http://www.unh.edu/rcm), Indiana University (http://weathertop.bry.indiana.edu/mas/rcm), University of Pennsylvania (http://www.finance.upenn.edu/comptroller/rcm), and University of Michigan (http://www.ur.umich.edu/9798/Nov26_97/budget.htm).

23. American Association of University Professors, "On Full-Time Non-Tenure-Track Appointments."

24. For instance, see the series of articles in American Association of University Professors, *Academe* 72, no. 4 (1986).

25. Kasper et al., "1986 Report on Full-Time Non-Tenure-Track Appointments"; "The Status of Non-Tenure-Track Faculty," *Academe: Bulletin of the AAUP* 79, no. 4 (1993): 39–46. See also American Association of University Professors, "Contingent Appointments and the Academic Profession" (the appendix reviews the AAUP statements and reports on the subject).

26. Association of American Universities, "Non-Tenure-Track Faculty Report" (Washington, DC: Association of American Universities, 2001).

27. Scott Smallwood, "After Three Years of Bargaining, U. of California Reaches Accord with Lecturers," *Chronicle of Higher Education*, June 20, 2003, A11; Scott Smallwood, "Non-Tenure-Track Faculty Members Vote to Unionize at U. of Michigan," *Chronicle of Higher Education*, May 9, 2003, A15.

28. Kay Mills, "New Life for U.S.C.: Prolific Fundraising Keys Big Changes in Recent Years," *National Crosstalk* 13, no. 3 (2005): 3–5.

29. Karen W. Arenson, "N.Y.U. Begins Hiring Effort to Lift Its Liberal Arts Standing," *New York Times*, September 27, 2004, 30L; Sexton, "The Role of Faculty in the Common Enterprise University."

30. University of Florida, *Academic Enhancement Program* (2007), available at http://www.president.ufl.edu/aep, accessed January 26, 2008; Tamar Lewin, "Public Universities Vie to Join the Top Ten in Academic Rankings," *New York Times*, December 20, 2006, A20.

31. Danny Hakim, "Spitzer Wants to Endow State's Public Colleges," *New York Times*, January 7, 2008, A21.

Chapter 4

1. Spellings Commission, "A Test of Leadership: Charting the Future of U.S. Higher Education" (Washington, DC: U.S. Department of Education, 2006); Charles Miller, "A Personal Letter," *National Crosstalk* (2006): 8A.

2. Philip H. Shelley, "Colleges Need to Give Students Intensive Care," *Chronicle of Higher Education*, January 5, 2005, B15.

3. Patricia J. Gumport, "Public Universities as Academic Workplaces," *Daedalus* 126, no. 4 (1997): 113–36.

4. Kelly Fields, "For-Profit Colleges Seek—and Find—New Allies among House Freshmen," *Chronicle for Higher Education*, April 11, 2008, A23.

5. Andrea L. Foster, "Illinois Plan to Draw 70,000 Students to Distance Education by 2018," *Chronicle of Higher Education*, April 27, 2007, A50. Other public flagship universities with a large online presence include Penn State University, with about 14,000 students taking classes online, and the University of Maryland, with 52,000 online students last year. Jodi S. Cohen, "U. of I. Taking Its Mission to Online Frontier," *Chicago Tribune*, September 8, 2006, A1.

6. Silla Brush, "College Dropouts Face Loan Hardships," *Chronicle of Higher Education*, May 13, 2005, A22; Greg Toppo, "College Graduates See Their Debt Burden Increase," *USA Today*, March 27, 2005, D1. Some public institutions have used declining state support as an effective argument to gain significant independence from state control. See the history of the Restructuring Act of 2005 on the University of Virginia website, available at http://www.virginia.edu/ restructuring, accessed September 10, 2008. Similar, although less dramatic, restructuring also occurred at the University of Washington.

7. D. C. Rogers, "Private Rates of Return to Education: A Case Study," *Yale Economic Essays* 9 (Spring 1969): 89–134; R. S. Eckaus, "Returns to Education with Standardized Incomes," *Quarterly Journal of Economics* 87 (1973): 121–31; George Psacharopoulos and Keith Hinchliffe, *Returns to Education: An International Comparison* (San Francisco: Jossey-Bass, 1973); Sebastian Pinera and Marcelo Selowsky, "The Opportunity Cost of Labor and the Returns to Education under Unemployment and Labor Market Segmentation," *Quarterly Journal of Economics* 92 (1978): 469–88.

8. See, e.g., Sandy Baum and Jennifer Ma, *Education Pays: The Benefits of Education for Individuals and Society* (Washington, DC: College Board Trends in Education Series, 2007).

9. See, e.g., Derek Bok, *Universities and the Future of America* (Cambridge: Harvard University Press, 1990); also see the publication produced by a group of Boston-area universities, available at http://www.bc.edu/offices/comaf/

economic/engines.html; Susan Hockfield, "Investing in the Nation's Future," *Boston Globe*, March 31, 2008, A11.

10. Although we are more diverse than we were, there remains much room for improvement in diversity in our nation's elite universities. Every one states a goal of improving diversity, which is underscored by the flurry of recent changes in financial aid programs that underwrite most costs of education for the nation's neediest students. The competition for the most talented of these students has become fierce. Those universities with large endowments are underwriting the total costs, something they can initially well afford since they have few such students on campus.

11. The nation's elite universities are more insulated from these pressures than are other institutions of higher education because their degrees are coveted by many. As long as applications increase and the quality of applicants stays high, there is less pressure to respond to the push for skills and vocational training. Nonetheless, we see some shift in choices of majors away from the humanities and toward business, engineering, and science.

12. Michelle Slatalla, "Cyberfamilias: Doing the Campus Hop," *New York Times*, April 10, 2008, G3.

13. For example, in 1998 economist Robert J. Barro was wooed by Columbia with a promise of a $300,000 annual salary, a reduced teaching load, and cushy office space. See Sylvia Naster, "Economics All-Star Says He Will Stay with the Home Team after All," *New York Times*, April 14, 1998, D1; Allison Schneider, "Recruiting Academic Stars: New Tactics in an Old Game," *Chronicle of Higher Education*, May 29, 1998, A12–14; Katherine Mangan, "A Shortage of Business Professors Leads to Six-Figure Salaries for New Ph.D.s," *Chronicle of Higher Education*, May 4, 2001, A12; Mark Levine, "Ivy Envy," *New York Times Magazine*, June 8, 2003, 72+.

14. James Monks and Ronald G. Ehrenberg, "*U.S. News & World Report's* College Rankings: Why Do They Matter?," *Change* 36, no. 6 (1999): 42–51.

15. Noel-Levitz, Inc., "Cost of Recruiting Report" (Iowa City: Noel-Levitz, Inc., 2006).

16. As Derek Bok has pointed out, the few stars in research universities earn high salaries, but the overall salaries in higher education, with few exceptions, have declined relative to salaries in other professions. Derek Bok, *Universities in the Marketplace: The Commercialization of Higher Education* (Princeton, NJ: Princeton University Press, 2003).

17. When universities employ world-famous political leaders or artists, they recognize that these NTT faculty contribute to their institution's visibility. These NTT faculty are often well paid.

18. A few interesting examples are described in Mary Taylor Huber, *Balancing Acts: The Scholarship of Teaching and Learning in Academic Careers* (Stanford: Carnegie Foundation for the Advancement of Teaching, 2004).

19. In 2008 Berkeley announced a huge "war chest" to fend off outside offers to its faculty. See "Berkeley Amasses $1.1 Billion 'War Chest' to Prevent Professor Poaching," in *The Chronicle of Higher Education News Blog*, March 14, 2008.

Chapter 5

1. Ehrenberg, Klaff, Keszbom, and Nagowski suggest such substitutability: "If graduate student unions . . . lead to substantially increased costs for the students, it is reasonable to expect that ultimately universities will reduce the size of their PhD programs and make more use of lecturers and other non-tenure-track faculty to staff undergraduate courses." See Ronald G. Ehrenberg, Daniel B. Klaff, Adam T. Keszbom, and Matthew P. Nagowski, "Collective Bargaining in American Higher Education," in Ronald G. Ehrenberg, ed., *Governing Academia* (Ithaca: Cornell University Press, 2004), 230.

2. Gnagey, "Provost"; "Renowned Engineer Joe C. Campbell Appointed to U. Va. Faculty."

3. Prior to 2000, Princeton's tenured and tenure-track faculty grew about 1 percent per year, without a corresponding increase in the size of the undergraduate student body. That was a major factor in the 2000 decision to embark on increasing the number of undergraduates in each class. However, Princeton has the largest endowment per student (over $2 million) of any university in the United States and is consequently in a unique position to invest in such an expensive undertaking. See Karen Arenson, "Big Spender," *New York Times*, April 20, 2008, 30L. We also acknowledge a private communication from Princeton.

4. American Association of University Professors, "Contingent Appointments and the Academic Profession."

5. Schuster and Finkelstein find that tenured faculty work effort has increased over time in all types of institutions, "although it has increased most dramatically at the research universities." Schuster and Finkelstein, *The American Faculty*, 79.

6. Schuster and Finkelstein report that NTT teaching-intensive faculty at research universities spend less time on work than TT faculty, perhaps as much as ten hours per week less. Schuster and Finkelstein, *The American Faculty*, 200.

7. Benjamin, *Exploring the Role of Contingent Instructional Staff in Undergraduate Learning*, 95–101.

8. Alexander Astin, *The American College Freshman: Thirty-Year Trends, 1966–1996* (Los Angeles: Higher Education Research Institute, UCLA, 1997).

9. The actual calculus used by economists for such a situation is not critical to our conclusion. The formal procedure considers the rewards to be obtained from a career that does not entail graduate education. It then compares those rewards

to those of a lottery whose cost is the time and expense of a graduate education and whose outcome is a probabilistically weighted mix of a possible tenured position or an alternative, perhaps tenure-track career. For some, the graduate education may be a sufficiently pleasant experience to offset its costs, but this fact does not alter the essential calculus.

10. Ronald Ehrenberg shows growing salary dispersion for tenured faculty between public and private institutions, across private universities and across fields within an institution. See Ronald G. Ehrenberg, "Studying Ourselves: The Academic Labor Market," *Journal of Labor Economics* 21, no. 2 (2003): 267–87.

11. American Association of University Professors, "Policy Documents and Reports" (Washington, DC: American Association of University Professors, 1995), 64.

12. Elia Powers, "Lawsuit against Princeton Comes into Focus," *Inside Higher Education*, October 26, 2007, available at http://www.insidehighered.com/news/2007/10/26/princeton, accessed September 10, 2008.

13. Cathy A. Trower, "Can Colleges Competitively Recruit Faculty without the Prospect of Tenure?," in Richard P. Chait, ed., *The Questions of Tenure* (Cambridge: Harvard University Press, 2002), 182–220.

14. Ibid., 201.

Chapter 6

1. Edie N. Goldenberg, "Undergraduate Education for Today and Tomorrow," Presidential Lecture Series on Academic Values (Ann Arbor: University of Michigan, 1993), 69–84.

2. Spellings Commission, "A Test of Leadership." We note that the word *tenure* appears nowhere in the body of that report.

3. In 2007, the University of California financed the development of a human resources assessment system to certify practices on its ten campuses, five medical schools, and two national laboratories. This was driven in part by unfavorable media attention and general dissatisfaction with personnel practices at the executive level. See National Academy of Public Administration, "University of California Certified Assessment of Human Resource Systems" (Washington, DC: National Academy of Public Administration, 2007).

4. See, for example, the following article and especially the series of comments posted to the online version: Scott Jaschik, "Das Ende for German at U.S.C.," *Inside Higher Education*, April 11, 2008, available at http://www.insidehighered.com/news/2008/04/11/german, accessed August 21, 2008.

5. Business models can work well on the business (nonacademic) side of universities. Providing unit incentives to reduce energy usage or to control space can reduce overall costs. However, these incentives exist under most traditional

incremental budgeting models as well. The observations that follow apply to the educational mission.

6. John Douglas Wilson argues that centralized incremental budgeting is superior to responsibility-centered management in raising educational quality. See John Douglas Wilson, "Tiebout Competition versus Political Competition on a University Campus," in Ehrenberg, *Governing Academia* (139–61).

7. David Kirp addresses RCM and other examples of this phenomenon in a number of elite research institutions. See David L. Kirp, *Shakespeare, Einstein and the Bottom Line: The Marketing of Higher Education* (Cambridge: Harvard University Press, 2003).

8. Paul W. Cook, "Decentralization and the Price-Transfer Problem," *Journal of Business* 28, no. 2 (1955): 87–94.

Chapter 7

1. Research universities with tenured faculty bargaining include Rutgers, Florida State, Temple, Wayne State, City University of New York, SUNY (Stonybrook and Buffalo), Universities of California (Santa Cruz), Cincinnati, Connecticut, Delaware, Florida, Hawaii, Massachusetts, and New Hampshire. We acknowledge a private communication from Ernst Benjamin of the American Association of University Professors.

2. In 1990, Debra Blum reported more than twenty decertifications after the *Yeshiva* decision. Debra Blum, "Ten Years after High Court Limited Faculty Bargaining, Merits of Academic Unionism Still Hotly Debated," *Chronicle of Higher Education*, January 31, 1990, A15+.

3. Scott Smallwood, "N.L.R.B. Rules against Faculty Union at Sage Colleges," *Chronicle of Higher Education*, August 17, 2001, A9.

4. The case of Point Park University provides an example. John Gravois, "Union Case Returned to Labor Board," *Chronicle of Higher Education*, August 11, 2006, A11.

5. Professors at the University of Minnesota threatened to organize a faculty union in affiliation with the AAUP in 1997 in response to a board initiative to reform tenure. In a close vote, the union lost. See Denise K. Magner, "U. of Minn. Faculty Rejects Union, Despite Battle with Regents," *Chronicle of Higher Education*, February 21, 1997, A11.

6. Drives to organize NTT faculty have taken place recently at New York University (with the UAW as the affiliated union); George Washington University (John Gravois, "Court Upholds Decision in Favor of Adjunct Union at George Washington U.," *Chronicle of Higher Education*, December 15, 2006, A9); The New School (John Gravois, "New School Adjuncts Get Union Contract," *Chronicle of Higher Education*, November 11, 2005, A13); Columbia College and Roosevelt University in Chicago; and Columbia University in New York City.

7. Ehrenberg et al., "Collective Bargaining in American Higher Education." Trower writes that "the outlook for doctoral graduates in geology, mathematics, economics, English, political science, and psychology was bleak compared to the academic labor market for chemistry, computer science, physics, business, history, and sociology." See Trower, "Can Colleges Competitively Recruit," 186.

8. In the late 1990s, the American Association for Higher Education (AAHE) sponsored the "Heeding New Voices" project that interviewed recently appointed faculty members from around the country. From those interviews, Eugene Rice reports that "the gulf between faculty and administrators" has widened and that faculty talked about a "social class gap" that they perceived between faculty and administrators in terms of salaries and lifestyles. If anything, those gaps have grown even larger in the last decade as salaries of presidents, provosts and deans have increased greatly. See R. Eugene Rice, "Making a Place for the New American Scholar," *New Pathways: Faculty Careers and Employment for the Twenty-first Century* (Washington, DC: American Association for Higher Education, 1996), 27.

9. See Ernst Benjamin, "Faculty Bargaining," in Ernst Benjamin and Michael Mauer, eds., *Academic Collective Bargaining* (23–51) (Washington, DC: American Association of University Professors and Modern Language Association, 2006).

10. Ibid.

11. Ehrenberg et al., "Collective Bargaining in American Higher Education," 209–33. The authors summarize the literature on the impact of collective bargaining on faculty salaries: "at best, faculty unions increase their members' average salaries by a very small percentage, and some found that faculty unions have had no effect." Ehrenberg et al., "Collective Bargaining in American Higher Education," 212.

12. For a discussion of collective bargaining approaches and agreements, see Ernst Benjamin and Michael Mauer, eds. *Academic Collective Bargaining* (Washington, DC: American Association of University Professors and Modern Language Association, 2006).

13. Trower found that one-year contacts were "particularly unattractive" for NTT faculty. Trower, "Can Colleges Competitively Recruit Faculty," 188.

14. Health coverage throughout the calendar year for NTT faculty is now standard practice in the research-centered universities in our study. We make no claim that it applies to other institutions that appoint non-tenure-track faculty.

15. Teachers in K–12 school systems share the same values with respect to their own students. An important difference, however, is that state regulations require a given number of class days and that any days lost to a strike are typically made up at the end of the year. That is, students do not lose class time when K–12 teachers strike.

Chapter 8

1. See Association of American Colleges, "Integrity in the College Curriculum: A Report to the Academic Community" (Washington, DC: Association of American Colleges, 1985); Miller, "A Personal Letter."

2. U.S. Department of Education, "Involvement in Learning: Realizing the Potential of American Higher Education" (Washington, DC: National Institute of Education, U.S. Department of Education, 1984); Gerald Bakker, "Making Teaching and Research Symbiotic," *Chronicle of Higher Education*, March 17, 1995, B3; Herbert W. Marsh and John Hattie, "The Relationship between Research Productivity and Teaching Effectiveness: Complementary, Antagonistic, or Independent Constructs?," *Journal of Higher Education* 73, no. 5 (2002): 603–04; Sexton, "The Role of Faculty in the Common Enterprise University"; Rosanna Breen, Roger Lindsay, and Alan Jenkins, *Reshaping Teaching in Higher Education: Linking Teaching with Research* (New York: Routledge, 2003).

3. Available at http://nsse.iub.edu/index.cfm.

4. Robert Zemsky, Susan Shaman, and Daniel B. Shapiro, *Higher Education as Competitive Enterprise: When Markets Matter* (San Francisco: Jossey-Bass, 2001): 55.

5. Ernest T. Pascarella and Patrick T. Terenzini, *How College Affects Students: Findings and Insights from Twenty Years of Research* (San Francisco: Jossey-Bass, 1991); Alexander W. Astin, *What Matters in College? Four Critical Years Revisited* (San Francisco: Jossey-Bass, 1993); Benjamin, "Declining Faculty Availability to Students Is the Problem—But Tenure Is Not the Explanation."

6. Ronald G. Ehrenberg and Liang Zhang, "Do Tenured and Tenure-Track Faculty Matter?," *Journal of Human Resources* 40, no. 3 (2005b): 647–59.

7. Astin, *What Matters in College? Four Critical Years Revisited*, 337–38.

8. Ibid., 412 (emphasis added).

9. Ibid., 412.

10. See, for example, Modern Language Association, "Ensuring the Quality of Undergraduate Programs in English and Foreign Languages: M.L.A. Recommendations on Staffing," *Profession 2002* (2002): 234–36; Ernst Benjamin, "How Over-Reliance on Contingent Appointments Diminishes Faculty Involvement in Student Learning," *Peer Review* (February 2002): 4–10. In a private communication, Benjamin also suggests that the casual way that NTT faculty members are hired, relative to the hiring of TT faculty, likely results in poorer teaching by NTT faculty. However, the criteria used in hiring TT faculty in premier research institutions have little to do with evidence of teaching effectiveness. In its November 9, 2003, statement on "Contingent Appointments and the Academic Profession," the American Association of University Professors writes that "It is the professional involvement of faculty in academic disciplines that ensures the quality, currency, and depth of the content being offered to students."

While TT faculty in research universities are deeply involved in their disciplines, NTT may also stay involved if their universities support professional development opportunities, including subsidized conference attendance. "A.A.U.P. Issues Statement on Use of Contingent Faculty Appointments," *Black Issues in Higher Education* 20, no. 17 (2003): 17.

11. Benjamin, "How Over-Reliance on Contingent Appointments Diminishes Faculty Involvement in Student Learning."

12. Exceptions that we know of include the Undergraduate Research Opportunities Program (UROP) at the University of Michigan and a recent initiative to evaluate research training of undergraduates at MIT.

13. Belton M. Fleisher, Bruce A. Weinberg, and Masanori Hashimoto, "Evaluating Methods for Evaluating Instruction: The Case of Higher Education," NBER Working Paper No. 12844 (Cambridge: National Bureau of Economic Research, 2007).

14. See Evan Jacobs and Anton S. Troianovsky, "C.U.E. Proposal Irks Some Faculty," *Harvard Crimson*, May 3, 2006, available at http://www.thecrimson .com/article.aspx?ref=513250; "Educating the Educators," *Harvard Crimson*, November 1, 2006, available at http://www.thecrimson.com/article.aspx?ref =515402.

15. After we disaggregate the data by department and level of instruction, we find that average evaluations by instructor type fall into a fairly narrow range— from 3.6 for chemistry to 4.8 for English. This means that differences of 0.3 or 0.4 can be statistically significant.

16. Benjamin, "Declining Faculty Availability to Students Is the Problem—but Tenure Is Not the Explanation."

17. Bettinger and Long find that graduate student teaching assistants are less proficient than either TT or NTT faculty as educators. Eric Bettinger and Bridget Terry Long, "Do College Instructors Matter? The Effects of Adjuncts and Graduate Assistants on Students' Interests and Success," NBER Working Paper No. 10370 (Cambridge: National Bureau of Economic Research, 2004).

18. Kenneth Feldman, "Grades and College Students' Evaluations of Their Courses and Teachers," *Research in Higher Education* 4, no. 1 (1976): 69–111; Lawrence Hamilton, "Grades, Class Size, and Faculty Status Predict Teaching Evaluations," *Teaching Sociology* 8, no. 1 (1980): 47–62; Melanie Moore and Richard Trahan, "Tenure Status and Grading Practices," *Sociological Perspectives* 41, no. 4 (1998): 775–81. A study of arts and sciences grades at Cornell shows that TT faculty grade harder than visitors, lecturers, and graduate students but that the differences are so small that they probably have no effect on evaluations. See Jay Parekh, "Do Median Grades Vary across Departments?," CHERI Working Paper No. 30 (Ithaca: Cornell Higher Education Research Institute, 2007). Teaching evaluations may also reflect totally irrelevant factors. Hamermesh and Parker present evidence that the physical appearance of instructors affects student evaluations. Daniel Hamermesh and Amy Parker, "Beauty in the

Classroom: Instructors' Pulchritude and Putative Pedagogical Productivity," *Economics of Education Review* 24, no. 4 (2005): 369–76.

19. Gary Burtless and Roger G. Noll, "Students and Research Universities," in Roger G. Noll, ed., *Challenges to Research Universities* (63–86) (Washington, DC: Brookings Institution, 1998); Cristina Gonzales, "Undergraduate Research, Graduate Mentoring, and the University's Mission," *Science* 293, no. 5535 (2001): 1624–26.

20. MIT launched the first such program in 1969 under the leadership of Margaret MacVicar, who subsequently became the first dean for undergraduate education at the Institute. In 1986, MacVicar was given the Charles A. Dana Award, a national award for educational innovation, for her leadership in the Undergraduate Research Opportunity Program.

21. The Council on Undergraduate Research, available at http://www.cur.org. See also the Undergraduate Research Community, available at http://www.kon .org/urc/undergrad_research.html, and Kerry K. Karukstis and Timothy E. Elgren, "Developing and Sustaining a Research-Supportive Curriculum: A Compendium of Successful Practices" (Washington, DC: Council on Undergraduate Research, 2007).

22. For example, MIT sends students around the world to work in government laboratories, private company laboratories, and universities through the MIT-Cambridge Exchange, the MIT International Science and Technology Initiatives (MISTI) Program, and the DC Policy Program. D-Lab (Design Laboratory) sends groups of students to developing countries to implement creative solutions to local problems.

23. American Mathematical Society Leadership Conference, Bloomington, Indiana, August 1999. Few of our ten universities monitor the availability of TT faculty to undergraduates through formal courses, research opportunities, or other activities. One exception is MIT. Every two years, each of the Corporation Visiting Committees to departments at MIT reviews trends in undergraduate enrollment and interviews groups of undergraduates. Because of this unusual system, a lack of interaction between TT faculty and undergraduates would be uncovered and addressed.

24. Faculty in laboratory science departments may prefer postdoctoral fellows to graduate students if graduate students cost more, but that is driven by wanting to stay competitive on proposals for grant funding and by wanting to hire the best trained assistants to advance research rather than by educational interests.

25. A number of graduate deans have the authority to determine the size of the graduate cohort that is admitted to each department and even the specific students admitted, but they rarely deny admission if the department wants the student and can provide funding. Public universities experience pressure from the state legislature to limit enrollments from out of state, but graduate students do not count. They are overwhelmingly from out of state as elite universities compete internationally for PhD applicants.

26. We still value tenure as a protection of academic freedom. In this, we disagree with views expressed by Peter Byrne and David Breneman (at least concerning colleges of arts and sciences) that adequate protections of academic freedom are possible without tenure. See Peter J. Byrne, *Academic Freedom without Tenure?*, New Pathways Working Paper Series no. 5 (Washington, DC: American Association for Higher Education, 1997), and David W. Breneman, *Alternatives to Tenure for the Next Generation of Academics*, New Pathways Series no. 14 (Washington, DC: American Association for Higher Education, 1997). Trower found that "Tenure track faculty and doctoral students believed that professional autonomy and academic freedom were greater on the tenure track" than in non-tenure-track positions. See Trower, "Can Colleges Recruit," 216.

Chapter 9

1. Trower and Honan found similar shortcomings in campus data systems of ten other institutions of higher education in 1999. See Cathy A. Trower and James P. Honan, "How Might Data Be Used?," in Richard P. Chait, ed., *The Questions of Tenure* (Cambridge: Harvard University Press, 2002), 273–308. They point to two cases in which tenure policy was under scrutiny by university boards and to the very different outcomes of those cases. They attribute a much more positive result in Arizona largely to having better information systems at Arizona than at Minnesota (273–76). In 2006, the University of California experienced a series of embarrassing newspaper revelations about the compensation and arrangements of various campus executives. After many taskforce reports, audits, and hearings, the board was urged to make changes, including investing in management information systems that would permit the board to monitor human resources practices on its campuses. This recommendation had been made years earlier but not implemented. National Academy of Public Administration, "University of California Certified Assessment of Human Resource Systems."

2. The subject of big-time athletics and their impact on universities has received an enormous amount of attention. For example, James Duderstadt, *Intercollegiate Athletics and the American University: A University President's Perspective* (Ann Arbor: University of Michigan Press, 2000). One way that competition in football, basketball, and hockey (the revenue-generating sports) affects the composition of the faculty is that athletes in those sports (but not in others) often require remedial courses and special tutoring provided by NTT faculty.

3. Trower relied on focus groups and a survey of advanced graduate students and young assistant professors in elite universities to identify what it would take to recruit talented individuals into NTT positions. See Trower, "Can Colleges Competitively Recruit?," 182–220.

4. Vannevar Bush, *Science: The Endless Frontier* (New York: Arno Press, 1980 [1945]).

5. Most senior faculty members at elite universities could not accurately describe graduation requirements for undergraduates or the different paths to completing them at their own institutions. Advising requires an understanding of elaborate rules and procedures, performance requirements, and other bureaucratic details that are rejected by most research-oriented faculty as irrelevant to anything that matters. Administration and advising matter to students and deans, and the people who specialize in them become indispensable to the effective functioning of the unit.

6. James Duderstadt has argued that the nation's elite research universities should get out of the business of undergraduate instruction entirely and focus instead on graduate training and research. James J. Duderstadt, *A University for the Twenty-first Century* (Ann Arbor: University of Michigan Press, 2000).

7. A few universities offer tenure to their specialists, using a review system that focuses heavily on achievements in the specialty area. For example, Princeton tenures research specialists. Michigan has tenured some teaching specialists. Also see Huber, *Balancing Acts*.

References

"AAUP Issues Statement on Use of Contingent Faculty Appointments." *Black Issues in Higher Education* 20, no. 17 (2003): 17.

American Association of University Professors. *AAUP Policy Documents and Reports*. 10th ed. Washington, DC: American Association of University Professors, 2006.

———. "Contingent Appointments and the Academic Profession." *AAUP Policy Documents and Reports* (10th ed., 98–114). Washington, DC: American Association of University Professors, 2006.

———. "1940 Statement of Principles on Academic Freedom and Tenure." Washington, DC: American Association of University Professors, 1940.

———. "On Full-Time Non-Tenure-Track Appointments." *AAUP Bulletin* 64, no. 3 1978: 267–73.

———. "Policy Documents and Reports." Washington, DC: American Association of University Professors, 1995.

American Council on Education. "The American College President." Washington, DC: American Council on Education, 2007.

American Council on Education. *American Colleges and Us*. Washington, DC: American Council on Education, 1973.

Anderson, Eugene L. "The New Professoriate: Characteristics, Contributions, and Compensation." Washington, DC: American Council on Education, Center for Policy Analysis, 2002.

Arenson, Karen. "Big Spender." *New York Times*, April 20, 2008, 30L.

———. "N.Y.U. Begins Hiring Effort to Lift Its Liberal Arts Standing." *New York Times*, September 27, 2004, B1.

Association of American Colleges. "Integrity in the College Curriculum: A Report to the Academic Community." Washington, DC: Association of American Colleges, 1985.

Association of American Universities. "Non-Tenure-Track Faculty Report." Washington, DC: Association of American Universities, 2001.

Association of Governing Boards of Universities and Colleges. "The Leadership Imperative: The Report of the A.G.B. Task Force on the State of the Presidency in American Higher Education." Washington, DC: Association of Governing Boards of Universities and Colleges, 2006.

Astin, Alexander W. *The American College Freshman: Thirty-Year Trends, 1966–1996*. Los Angeles: Higher Education Research Institute, UCLA, 1997.

Astin, Alexander W. *What Matters in College? Four Critical Years Revisited*. San Francisco: Jossey-Bass, 1993.

Bakker, Gerald. "Making Teaching and Research Symbiotic." *Chronicle of Higher Education*, March 17, 1995, B3.

Baldwin, Roger G., and Jay L. Chronister. *Teaching without Tenure: Policies and Practices for a New Era*. Baltimore: Johns Hopkins University Press, 2001.

Barnetson, B. "Part-Time and Limited-Term Faculty in Alberta's Colleges." *Canadian Journal of Higher Education* 31, no. 2 (2001): 79–102.

Baum, Sandy, and Jennifer Ma. *Education Pays: The Benefits of Education for Individuals and Society*. Washington, DC: College Board Trends in Education Series, 2007.

Benjamin, Ernst. "Changing Distribution of Faculty by Tenure Status and Gender." Memorandum to AAUP Executive Committee, January 29, 1997.

———. "Declining Faculty Availability to Students Is the Problem—But Tenure Is Not the Explanation." *American Behavioral Scientist* 41, no. 5 (1998): 716–35.

———. *Exploring the Role of Contingent Instructional Staff in Undergraduate Learning*. San Francisco: Jossey-Bass, 2003.

———. "Faculty Bargaining." In Ernst Benjamin and Michael Mauer, eds., *Academic Collective Bargaining* (23–51). Washington, DC: American Association of University Professors and Modern Language Association, 2006.

———. "How Over-Reliance on Contingent Appointments Diminishes Faculty Involvement in Student Learning." *Peer Review* (February 2002): 4–10.

Benjamin, Ernst, and Michael Mauer, eds. *Academic Collective Bargaining*. Washington, DC: American Association of University Professors and Modern Language Association, 2006.

Bettinger, Eric, and Bridget Terry Long. "Do College Instructors Matter? The Effects of Adjuncts and Graduate Assistants on Students' Interests and Success." NBER Working Paper No. 10370, Cambridge, MA: National Bureau of Economic Research, 2004.

Blum, Debra. "Ten Years after High Court Limited Faculty Bargaining, Merits of Academic Unionism Still Hotly Debated." *Chronicle of Higher Education*, January 31, 1990, A15+.

Blumenstyk, Goldie. "Outside Chance for Insiders: Unlike Most Leading Businesses, Colleges Favor External Candidates for Their Top Jobs." *Chronicle of Higher Education*, November 4, 2005, 8.

Bok, Derek. *Universities and the Future of America*. Cambridge: Harvard University Press, 1990.

———. *Universities in the Marketplace: The Commercialization of Higher Education*. Princeton: Princeton University Press, 2003.

Borjas, George. "Foreign-Born Teaching Assistants and the Academic Performance of Undergraduates." *American Economic Review* 90, no. 2 (2000): 355–59.

Boston College. "Engines of Economic Growth." Boston College, 2007. Available at http://www.bc.edu/offices/comaf/economic/engines.html, accessed September 10, 2008.

Bousquet, Marc. " 'We Are Teachers, Hear Us Roar': Contingent Faculty Author an Activist Culture." *Cinema Journal* 45, no. 4 (2006): 97–107.

Bousquet, Marc, Tony Scott, and Leo Parascondola. *Tenured Bosses and Disposable Teachers: Writing Instruction in the Managed University*. Carbondale: Southern Illinois University Press, 2004.

Bradley, Gwendolyn. "Contingent Faculty and the New Academic Labor System: To Defend Academic Values, We Need to Roll Back the Reliance on Contingent Labor." *Academe: Bulletin of the AAUP* 90, no. 1 (2004): 28.

Breen, Rosanna, Roger Lindsay, and Alan Jenkins. *Reshaping Teaching in Higher Education: Linking Teaching with Research*. New York: Routledge, 2003.

Breneman, David W. *Alternatives to Tenure for the Next Generation of Academics*. New Pathways Series no. 14. Washington, DC: American Association for Higher Education, 1997.

Brinkman, Paul. "Responsibility Center Budgeting: An Approach to Decentralized Management for Institutions of Higher Education." *Planning for Higher Education* 21 (1993): 49–51.

Brumi, Andrew. "Freshmen Overload U.R." *Campus Times*, September 14, 2006, 1.

Brush, Silla. "College Dropouts Face Loan Hardships." *Chronicle of Higher Education*, May 13, 2005, A22.

Buck, Jane. "Features: The President's Report. Successes, Setbacks, and Contingent Labor: Can Higher Education Thrive When Part-Time Faculty Do Most of the Teaching?" *Academe: Bulletin of the AAUP* 87, no. 5 (2001): 18.

Burtless, Gary, and Roger G. Noll. "Students and Research Universities." In Roger G. Noll, ed., *Challenges to Research Universities* (63–86). Washington, DC: Brookings Institution, 1998.

Bush, Vannevar. *Science: The Endless Frontier.* New York: Arno Press, 1980 [1945].

Byrne, Peter J. *Academic Freedom without Tenure?* New Pathways Working Paper Series no. 5. Washington, DC: American Association for Higher Education, 1997.

Caison, Amy L. "Tenure Trends in Public, Four-Year Colleges and Universities." *Planning for Higher Education* 31, no. 2 (2003): 15–25.

Carnegie Foundation for the Advancement of Teaching. *Reinventing Undergraduate Education: A Blueprint for America's Universities.* Stony Brook: State University of New York, 1998.

Chait, Richard, ed. *The Questions of Tenure.* Cambridge: Harvard University Press, 2002.

Cohen, Jodi S. "U. of I. Taking Its Mission to Online Frontier." *Chicago Tribune,* September 8, 2006, A1.

Cohen, Michael D., and James G. March. *Leadership and Ambiguity: The American College President.* New York: McGraw-Hill, 1974.

Cook, Paul W. "Decentralization and the Price-Transfer Problem." *Journal of Business* 28, no. 2 (1955): 87–94.

Council on Undergraduate Education. Website at: http://www.cur.org. Accessed August 26, 2008.

Duderstadt, James J. *Intercollegiate Athletics and the American University: A University President's Perspective.* Ann Arbor: University of Michigan Press, 2000.

Duderstadt, James J. *A University for the Twenty-first Century.* Ann Arbor: University of Michigan Press, 2000.

Duncan, John C. "The Indentured Servants of Academia: The Adjunct Faculty Dilemma and Their Limited Legal Remedies." *Indiana Law Journal* 74, no. 2 (1999): 513–86.

Eckaus, R. S. "Returns to Education with Standardized Incomes." *Quarterly Journal of Economics* 87 (1973): 121–31.

"Educating the Educators." *Harvard Crimson,* November 1, 2006. Available at http://www.thecrimson.com/article.aspx?ref=515402, accessed August 19, 2008.

Ehrenberg, Ronald G. "Studying Ourselves: The Academic Labor Market." *Journal of Labor Economics* 21, no. 2 (2003): 267–87.

Ehrenberg, Ronald G., Daniel B. Klaff, Adam T. Keszbom, and Matthew P. Nagowski. "Collective Bargaining in American Higher Education." In Ronald G. Ehrenberg, ed., *Governing Academia* (209–33). Ithaca: Cornell University Press, 2004.

Ehrenberg, Ronald G., and Liang Zhang. "The Changing Nature of Faculty Employment." In Robert Clark and Jennifer Ma, eds., *Recruitment, Retention, and Retirement in Higher Education* (32–50). Northhampton, MA: Edward Elgar, 2005.

———. "Do Tenured and Tenure-Track Faculty Matter?" *Journal of Human Resources* 40, no. 3 (2005): 647–59.

Feldman, Daniel C., and William H. Turnley. "Contingent Employment in Academic Careers: Relative Deprivation among Adjunct Faculty." *Journal of Vocational Behavior* 64, no. 2 (2004): 284–307.

Feldman, Kenneth. "Grades and College Students' Evaluations of Their Courses and Teachers." *Research in Higher Education* 4, no. 1 (1976): 69–111.

Fields, Kelly. "For-Profit Colleges Seek—and Find—New Allies among House Freshmen." *Chronicle of Higher Education*, April 11, 2008, A23.

Finkelstein, Martin J., and Jack H. Schuster. "Assessing the Silent Revolution: How Changing Demographics Are Reshaping the Academic Profession." *AAHE Bulletin* 54, no. 2 (2001): 3–7.

Fleisher, Belton M., Bruce A. Weinberg, and Masanori Hashimoto. "Evaluating Methods for Evaluating Instruction: The Case of Higher Education." NBER Working Paper No. 12844. Cambridge: National Bureau of Economic Research, 2007.

Fogg, Piper. "For These Professors, 'Practice' Is Perfect." *Chronicle of Higher Education*, April 16, 2004, A12.

———. "Teaching Your Way to Tenure." *Chronicle of Higher Education*, September 1, 2006, A18.

Foster, Andrea L. "Illinois Plan to Draw 70,000 Students to Distance Education by 2018." *Chronicle of Higher Education,* April 27, 2007, A50.

Gappa, Judith M. "Off the Tenure Track: Six Models for Full-Time, Non-tenurable Appointments." New Pathways Working Paper Series, Inquiry No. 10. Washington, DC: American Association for Higher Education, 1996.

Gappa, Judith M., and David W. Leslie. *The Invisible Faculty: Improving the Status of Part-Timers in Higher Education.* San Francisco: Jossey-Bass, 1993.

Gnagey, Laurel Thomas. "Provost: Hiring of One Hundred New Faculty Set to Begin." *University of Michigan Record*, January 25, 2008. Available at http://www.ur.umich.edu/0708/Jan21_08/04.shtml, accessed September 10, 2008.

Goldenberg, Edie N. "Undergraduate Education for Today and Tomorrow." Presidential Lecture Series on Academic Values. Ann Arbor: University of Michigan, 1993.

Gonzales, Cristina. "Undergraduate Research, Graduate Mentoring, and the University's Mission." *Science* 293, no. 5535 (2001): 1624–26.

Gravois, John. "Court Upholds Decision in Favor of Adjunct Union at George Washington U." *Chronicle of Higher Education*, December 15, 2006, A9.

———. "Legislative Campaign Pushed by AFT." *Chronicle of Higher Education*, April 13, 2007, A13.

————. "New School Adjuncts Get Union Contract." *Chronicle of Higher Education*, November 11, 2005, A13.

————. "Union Case Returned to Labor Board." *Chronicle of Higher Education*, August 11, 2006, A11.

Gumport, Patricia J. "Public Universities as Academic Workplaces." *Daedalus* 126, no. 4 (1997): 113–36.

Hakim, Danny. "Spitzer Wants to Endow State's Public Colleges." *New York Times*, January 7, 2008, A21.

Hamermesh, Daniel, and Amy Parker. "Beauty in the Classroom: Instructors' Pulchritude and Putative Pedagogical Productivity." *Economics of Education Review* 24, no. 4 (2005): 369–76.

Hamilton, Lawrence. "Grades, Class Size, and Faculty Status Predict Teaching Evaluations." *Teaching Sociology* 8, no. 1 (1980): 47–62.

Herman, Deborah M., and Julie M. Schmid. *Cogs in the Classroom Factory: The Changing Identity of Academic Labor*. Westport, CT: Praeger, 2003.

Hess, John. "The Entrepreneurial Adjunct: Contingent Faculty Become Commodities in the New Academic Labor Market." *Academe: Bulletin of the AAUP* 90, no. 1 (2004): 37.

Hockfield, Susan. "Investing in the Nation's Future." *Boston Globe*, March 31, 2008, A11.

Horowitz, David. *The Professors: The One Hundred One Most Dangerous Academics in America*. Washington, DC: Regnery, 2006.

Huber, Mary Taylor. *Balancing Acts: The Scholarship of Teaching and Learning in Academic Careers*. Stanford: Carnegie Foundation for the Advancement of Teaching, 2004.

Jacobe, Monica F. "Contingent Faculty across the Disciplines: News on the Non-Tenure-Track Front." *Academe: Bulletin of the AAUP* 92, no. 6 (2006): 43.

Jacobs, Evan, and Anton S. Troianovsky. "C.U.E. Proposal Irks Some Faculty." *Harvard Crimson*, May 3, 2006. Available at http://www.thecrimson.com/article.aspx?ref=513250, accessed August 19, 2008.

Jacobs, Frederic. "Using Part-Time Faculty More Effectively." *New Directions for Higher Education* 1998, no. 104 (1998): 9–18.

Jaschik, Scott. "Das Ende for German at U.S.C." *Inside Higher Education*, April 11, 2008. Available at http://www.insidehighered.com/news/2008/04/11/german, accessed August 19, 2008.

Johnson, Benjamin, Patrick Kavanagh, and Kevin Mattson. *Steal This University: The Rise of the Corporate University and the Academic Labor Movement*. New York: Routledge, 2003.

Kafka, Franz. *The Castle*. Trans. Willa and Edwin Muir. New York: Knopf, 1964.

Karukstis, Kerry K., and Timothy E. Elgren. "Developing and Sustaining a Research-Supportive Curriculum: A Compendium of Successful Practices." Washington, DC: Council on Undergraduate Research, 2007.

Kasper, H., F. Bronner, M. W. Gray, B. R. Kreiser, and J. R. Rosenthal. "1986 Report on Full-Time Non-Tenure-Track Appointments." *Academe: Bulletin of the AAUP* 72, no. 4 (1986): A14–A19.

Kirp, David L. *Shakespeare, Einstein and the Bottom Line: The Marketing of Higher Education.* Cambridge: Harvard University Press, 2003.

Leatherman, Courtney. "Part-Timers Continue to Replace Full-Timers on College Faculties." *Chronicle of Higher Education*, January 28, 2000, A18.

Levine, Mark. "Ivy Envy." *New York Times Magazine*, June 8, 2003, 72+.

Lewin, Tamar. "Public Universities Vie to Join the Top Ten in Academic Rankings." *New York Times*, December 20, 2006, A20.

Liu, Xiangmin, and Liang Zhang. "What Determines Employment of Part-Time Faculty in Higher Education Institutions?" CHERI Working Paper No. 105. Ithaca: Cornell Higher Education Research Institute, 2007.

Low, Lana. "Are College Students Satisfied? A National Analysis of Changing Expectations." New Agenda Series, Iowa City: Noel-Levitz, Inc., 2000.

MacKenna, E. "Contingent Performances: Between the Acts of Adjunct Faculty." *Journal of the Midwest Modern Language Association* 37, no. 2 (2004): 45–48.

Mangan, Katherine. "A Shortage of Business Professors Leads to Six-Figure Salaries for New Ph.D.s." *Chronicle of Higher Education*, May 4, 2001, A12.

Marsh, Herbert W., and John Hattie. "The Relationship between Research Productivity and Teaching Effectiveness: Complementary, Antagonistic, or Independent Constructs?" *Journal of Higher Education* 73, no. 5 (2002): 603–41.

Martucci, Brian. "Unexpectedly High Yield Brings Large Class of '10." *The Mac Weekly*, March 3, 2006, 1.

Massy, William F. "Measuring Performance: How Colleges and Universities Can Set Meaningful Goals." In William F. Massy and Joel W. Meyerson, eds., *Measuring Institutional Performance in Higher Education* (29–54). Princeton: Peterson's, 1994.

Miller, Charles. "A Personal Letter." *National Crosstalk* 14, no. 4 (2006): 8A.

Mills, Kay. "New Life for U.S.C.: Prolific Fundraising Keys Big Changes in Recent Years." *National Crosstalk* 13, no. 3 (2005): 3–5.

Modern Language Association. "Ensuring the Quality of Undergraduate Programs in English and Foreign Languages: M.L.A. Recommendations on Staffing." *Profession 2002* (2002): 234–36.

Monks, James. "The Relative Earnings of Contingent Faculty in Higher Education." *Journal of Labor Research* 28, no. 3 (2007): 487–501.

Monks, James, and Ronald G. Ehrenberg. "*U.S. News & World Report's* College Rankings: Why Do They Matter." *Change* 36, no. 6 (1999): 42–51.

Moore, Melanie, and Richard Trahan. "Tenure Status and Grading Practices." *Sociological Perspectives* 41, no. 4 (1998): 775–81.

Murphy, Michael. "Adjuncts Should Not Just Be Visitors in the Academic Promised Land." *Chronicle of Higher Education*, March 29, 2002, B14.

Naster, Sylvia. "Economics All-Star Says He Will Stay with the Home Team after All." *New York Times*, April 14, 1998, D1.

National Academy of Public Administration. "University of California Certified Assessment of Human Resource Systems." Washington, DC: National Academy of Public Administration, 2007.

Nelson, Cary. *Will Teach for Food: Academic Labor in Crisis.* Minneapolis: University of Minnesota Press, 1997.

Nelson, Cary, and Stephen Watt. *Office Hours: Activism and Change in the Academy.* New York: Routledge, 2004.

Noel-Levitz, Inc. "Cost of Recruiting Report." Iowa City: Noel-Levitz, Inc., 2006.

Ohio State University. *E. Gordon Gee, President: Biography.* The Ohio State University (2008). Available at http://president.osu.edu/bio.php, accessed January 26, 2008.

Padilla, Art, and Sujit Ghosh. "Turnover at the Top: The Revolving Door of the Academic Presidency." *Presidency* 3, no. 1 (2000): 30–37.

Parekh, Jay. "Do Median Grades Vary across Departments?" CHERI Working Paper No. 30. Ithaca: Cornell Higher Education Research Institute, 2003.

Pascarella, Ernest T., and Patrick T. Terenzini. *How College Affects Students: Findings and Insights from Twenty Years of Research.* San Francisco: Jossey-Bass, 1991.

Pinera, Sebastian, and Marcelo Selowsky. "The Opportunity Cost of Labor and the Returns to Education under Unemployment and Labor Market Segmentation." *Quarterly Journal of Economics* 92 (1978): 469–488.

Powers, Elia. "Lawsuit against Princeton Comes into Focus," *Inside Higher Education*, October 26, 2007. Available at http://www.insidehighered.com/news/2007/10/26/princeton, accessed September 10, 2008.

Psacharopoulos, George, and Keith Hinchliffe. *Returns to Education: An International Comparison.* San Francisco: Jossey-Bass, 1973.

"Quit Hiring Short-Term, Tenure Track Profs Needed." *Indiana Daily Student*, April 26, 2002, 8.

"Reinventing Undergraduate Education: Three Years After the Boyer Report." Miami: The Boyer Commission on Educating Undergraduates in the Research University, 2002. Available at http://www.reinventioncenter.miami.edu/BoyerSurvey/index.html#survey01, accessed September 10, 2008.

"Renowned Engineer Joe C. Campbell Appointed to U. Va. Faculty." *University of Virginia News Services*, June 13, 2005. Available at http://www.virginia.edu/topnews/releases2005/campbell-june-13-2005.html, accessed August 19, 2008.

Rhoades, Gary. *Managed Professionals: Unionized Faculty and Restructuring Academic Labor, SUNY Series, Frontiers in Education.* Albany: State University of New York Press, 1998.

———. "Reorganizing the Faculty Workforce for Flexibility: Part-Time Professional Labor." *Journal of Higher Education* 67, no. 6 (1996): 626–60.

Rice, R. Eugene. "Making a Place for the New Academic Scholar." *New Pathways: Faculty Careers and Employment for the Twenty-first Century.* Washington, DC: American Association for Higher Education 1996.

Rimer, Sara. "Harvard Task Force Calls for New Focus on Teaching and Not Just Research." *New York Times*, May 10, 2007, A20.

Robinson, Ian, and David Dobbie. "Reorganizing Higher Education in the United States and Canada: The Erosion of Tenure and the Unionization of Contingent Faculty." *Labor Studies Journal* 33, no. 2 (2008): 117–40.

Rogers, D. C. "Private Rates of Return to Education: A Case Study." *Yale Economic Essays* 9 (Spring 1969): 89–134.

Schneider, Allison. "Recruiting Academic Stars: New Tactics in an Old Game." *Chronicle of Higher Education*, May 29, 1998, A12–A14.

Schuster, Jack H., and Martin J. Finkelstein. *The American Faculty: The Restructuring of Academic Work and Careers.* Baltimore: Johns Hopkins University Press, 2006.

Sexton, John. "The Role of Faculty in the Common Enterprise University." Report to the Trustees Council of New York University. New York: New York University.

Shelley, Philip H. "Colleges Need to Give Students Intensive Care." *Chronicle of Higher Education,* January 5, 2005, B15.

Slatalla, Michelle. "Cyberfamilias: Doing the Campus Hop." *New York Times*, April 10, 2008, G3.

Slaughter, Sheila, and Gary Rhoades. *Academic Capitalism and the New Economy: Markets, State, and Higher Education.* Baltimore: Johns Hopkins University Press, 2004.

Smallwood, Scott. "After Three Years of Bargaining, U. of California Reaches Accord with Lecturers." *Chronicle of Higher Education*, June 20, 2003, A11.

———. "Disappearing Act: The Invisible Adjunct Shuts Down Her Popular Weblog and Says Goodbye to Academe." *Chronicle of Higher Education*, April 30, 2004, A10–A11.

———. "Faculty Activists across North America Rally for Better Treatment of Part-Timers." *Chronicle of Higher Education*, October 30, 2001. Available at http://chronicle.com/daily/2001/10/2001103006n.htm, accessed on August 19, 2008.

————. "N.L.R.B. Rules against Faculty Union at Sage Colleges." *Chronicle of Higher Education*, August 17, 2001, A9.

————. "Non-Tenure-Track Faculty Members Vote to Unionize at U. of Michigan." *Chronicle of Higher Education*, May 9, 2003, A15.

Spellings Commission. *A Test of Leadership: Charting the Future of U.S. Higher Education*. Washington, DC: U.S. Department of Education, 2006.

"The Status of Non-Tenure-Track Faculty." *Academe: Bulletin of the AAUP* 79, no. 4 (1993): 39–46.

Strauss, Jon C., and John R. Curry. *Responsibility Center Management: Lessons from Twenty-five Years of Decentralized Management*. Annapolis Junction, MD: National Association of College and University Business Officials, 2002.

Sullivan, Brian K. "Yale May Expand Enrollment as Levin Sees Ivy League Competition." *Bloomberg News Service*, August 30, 2007. Available at http://www.bloomberg.com/apps/news?pid=newsarchive&sid=aH1kNjCfOzVE, accessed August 19, 2008.

Thompson, Karen. "Contingent Faculty and Student Learning: Welcome to the Strativersity." *New Directions for Higher Education* 2003, no. 123 (2003): 41.

Tierney, William G. "Tenure Is Dead. Long Live Tenure." In William G. Tierney, ed., *The Responsive University: Restructuring for High Performance* (38–61). Baltimore: Johns Hopkins University Press, 1998.

Toppo, Greg. "College Graduates See Their Debt Burden Increase." *USA Today*, March 27, 2005, D1.

Trower, Cathy A. "Can Colleges Competitively Recruit Faculty without the Prospect of Tenure?" In Richard P. Chait, ed., *The Questions of Tenure* (182–220). Cambridge: Harvard University Press, 2002.

Trower, Cathy A., and James P. Honan. "How Might Data Be Used?" In Richard P. Chait, ed., *The Questions of Tenure* (273–308). Cambridge: Harvard University Press, 2002.

Umbach, P. D. "How Effective Are They? Exploring the Impact of Contingent Faculty on Undergraduate Education." *Review of Higher Education* 30, no. 2 (2007): 91+.

United States Department of Education. "Involvement in Learning: Realizing the Potential of American Higher Education." Washington, DC: National Institute of Education, U.S. Department of Education, 1984.

"University of California Certified Assessment of Human Resource Systems." Washington, DC: National Academy of Public Administration, 2007.

University of Florida. "Academic Enhancement Program." University of Florida, 2007. Available at http://www.president.ufl.edu/aep, accessed January 26, 2008.

University of Virginia. "Higher Education Restructuring." University of Virginia, 2008. Available at http://www.virginia.edu/restructuring/, accessed September 10, 2008.

VanderMay, Anne. " 'U' Overshoots Enrollment Targets Again." *Michigan Daily*, October 27, 2005, A1+.

Whalen, Edward. *Responsibility Center Budgeting: An Approach to Decentralized Management for Institutions of Higher Education*. Bloomington: Indiana University Press, 1991.

Whitaker, Gilbert R. "Value Centered Management: The Michigan Approach to Responsibility Center Management." *The University Record*, January 9, 1995, NA.

Wilson, John Douglas. "Tiebout Competition versus Political Competition on a University Campus." In Ronald G. Ehrenberg, ed., *Governing Academia* (139–61). Ithaca: Cornell University Press, 2004.

Wilson, Robin. "U. of North Florida to Replace Forty-six Adjunct Faculty Members to Meet Accreditor's Criteria." *Chronicle of Higher Education*, October 30, 2001. Available at http://chronicle.com/daily/2001/10/2001103007n.htm, accessed August 19, 2008.

Wilson, Robin. "Tales of the Reconstruction: Can Reorganization Save the AAUP?" *Chronicle of Higher Education*, June 27, 2008, A4.

Winston, Gordon. "The Necessary Revolution in Financial Accounting." *Planning for Higher Education* 20, no. 4 (1992): 1–15.

Wolf, Barbara, Michael Burnham, Andrea Tuttle Kornbluh, and Eliza Combs. *A Simple Matter of Justice*. Disk 2, *Contingent Faculty Organize*. Cincinnati: Barbara Wolf Video Work, 2001.

Zemsky, Robert, Susan Shaman, and Daniel B. Shapiro. *Higher Education as Competitive Enterprise: When Markets Matter*. San Francisco: Jossey-Bass, 2001.

Index